MW01138078

Gaslighting

The Complete Guide to Identifying, Handling & Avoiding Manipulation.

Recover from Emotional Abuse and Build Healthy Relationships

Linda Hill

Gaslighting

Gaslighting

Table of Contents

Your Free Gift

As a way of saying thanks for your purchase, I want to offer you a free bonus e-Book called How to Say "No", exclusive to readers of this book.

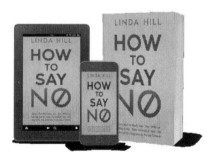

In this book you'll discover:

- How to say "no" without feeling guilty or hurting other's feelings
- How to quit people pleasing and stand up for yourself
- How to distinguish between being a helpful person and being a doormat
- And so much more

If you finally want to end people pleasing for good, then grab this book.

To get instant access, just go to:

<u>PeakPublishBooks.com/people</u>

Or Scan the QR Code below:

Introduction

Understanding gaslighting is perhaps one of the biggest obstacles victims—and humanity in general—fight with; and the reason this is such a problem is because gaslighting deals in human emotions. Gaslighting is a very tricky form of abuse, as it is not only the words that are spoken, but also how those words are used to abuse the victim's sense of their own perception and emotions. On top of that, personal perception and emotions are already something that many people have problems with; it is not uncommon for a person who has not experienced gaslighting, to experience doubt or confusion about their feelings or awareness of scenarios within their own circle. Being able to clearly identify your own emotions, pinpoint why they are occurring, and healthily relaying all of that information in an informative (rather than accusatory) manner to the person who has incited those feelings, takes skill, practice, and a lot of emotional and psychological know-how.

Something that many of us are striving to achieve, but have a long way to reach.

However, that is by no means a dismissal of the feelings you are currently feeling or wondering in relation to your own circumstances. Instead, take the above comments as the beginnings of foundational knowledge. In order to clearly determine if you are being gaslighted, you are going to have to be open to understanding your feelings, identifying why you feel a certain way, and ready to put that into a hindsight perspective.

Something you will have to come to terms with in order to move forward is that fighting, understanding, and avoiding gaslighting are going to be a long stretch of your mental health journey; and while this book will help you with beginning that journey, it will be a lot longer than simply finishing reading and mentally being aware of what this book brings up. It is going to require you to be accountable to yourself and others on how you actively intend to heal yourself. But do not worry, this book will give you key guidelines on how to become active with your healing, and how to find the people to help you.

Before going forward into the nitty-gritty of how gaslighting works, there are some specific words we'll use that you should know.

Terms

In the examples given throughout this book, you may encounter terms with which you are not familiar, so they are going to be explained now.

The Flags

Remember as a child when there was a game called "green flag, yellow flag, red flag"? Perhaps not, it could be a niche childhood game. Regardless as to whether or not you remember it, similar to traffic lights, the terms "green flag", "yellow flag" and "red flag" can also refer to emotional responses within yourself to the world around you.

Red Flags

Red flags, just like red lights, are a big problem where you have to 'stop'. When it comes to interpersonal relationships, or even the relationship you have with yourself, a red flag symbolizes something that is wrong and must be dealt with as soon as possible. One great example would be physical abuse. If you, or someone you know, is being abused then there is no time to waste—you must make a plan and either ask for help, or help the person you know.

Some of you might be wondering: "This book is about gaslighting, how did we jump all the way to physical abuse?" Well, first off, in some cases there is not as big of a gap between the two as many might think. The two could actually be next-door neighbors, but that is a case-by-case scenario, and is something that you and your loved ones should monitor closely. Second, physical abuse is something that basically everyone in society—aside from the actual abuser and their cohorts—will agree is inherently wrong. Predominantly, red flags fall into this type of category.

Yellow Flags

Yellow flags, as with yellow lights, are where things get tricky. To some, these actions are red flags, and to others, this is the gray area of relationships. When it comes to yellow flags the choice is ultimately up to you and how you want the relationship or scenario to continue. For example, in a normal dating relationship, if two young adults (before their thirties) begin to date, there are many socially and culturally-based yellow flags such as: drinking, friend groups, living situations, ownership of transportation, jobs, etc. In these scenarios it is up to the couple, or one person in the couple, to decide what they are able to live with currently, and what is a deal-breaker—and that often happens over time.

The trickiness of yellow flags then becomes twofold. First, they are based on an individual's character, their specific relationship with someone else, and their desires or goals for that relationship; all of which are relatively fluid concepts depending on the other person, the time in each individual's lives, and their respective goals and how they fit into each other, if at all. Second, yellow flags tend to resolve themselves over time. Many problems that are yellow flag based are things that are not entirely actionable right away.

For example, say that your friend got a new job that they had really wanted, but they did not like a particular coworker for no other reason than their personalities just did not mix (this coworker was not toxic, lazy, or incompetent—in fact, outside of the personality differences the two were becoming a dynamic duo at work). Would you encourage your friend to quit? Most likely not. Instead, most people would encourage that friend to either find a compromise, or try to get to know that person a little better. In this scenario, there is a very good chance that after a little while, while the two may never become best friends, their working relationship would improve and create more productivity (please note that it is not always the case and is really subjective to multiple outside factors).

The problem with yellow flags is that since they often take time to be resolved, they are one of the key components of how a gaslighter is able to sneak into someone's life. Gaslighting is a form of emotional abuse and, therefore, concerns emotions and perception of emotions—which as previously stated, are a mental minefield on a good day—making the ability to pinpoint the exact traits of a gaslighter without incredibly good personal intuition or training, incredibly difficult. Allowing a gaslighter into your life is not a sign that you are non-perceptive, weak, or anything of the kind. It simply means that they were too sneaky for you to notice, you were too kind and permissive for too long, or those little inklings in your gut of "something is wrong," were not strong enough to cause you to leave sooner. What matters is that you are seeking help now.

Back to yellow flags—not every yellow flag means that the person is a gaslighter. But on the other hand, that does not signify the yellow flags you perceive in your life to not be a form of gaslighting.

See the trickiness of it?

Green Flags

For the most part, green flags do not need an interpretation. These represent things in your relationship that you are all-for. Open and honest communication, willingness to accept responsibility for their actions, following-through with promises—whatever these things are, the green flags are probably why you are in that relationship.

Small Note

It is important to note that many relationships have a small combination of yellow and green flags. In fact, that is perfectly normal. It is even normal to acknowledge that a gaslighter has some green flags. Many gaslighters are unintentional gaslighters, as they probably learned it from a systemic background, like their own families. But that does not mean it is okay for them to continue to be a gaslighter, or to gaslight their partners, friends, or loved ones.

When figuring out your own emotions and relationships, it is okay to acknowledge the good, even if it is only two percent of the whole. The problem is when you allow that small percentage of good to keep you in a predominantly bad or harmful scenario.

Safe People

"Safe people" is a term for people in your life that you can completely trust, be authentic with, and who will not judge you or make you feel bad for your feelings. Additionally, these people never cause you to question their respect for you, or have never caused you to question their authenticity in their care and advice. These people take many forms: they could be your parents, mentors, or someone that you just connected with. However you find them, these people are most likely the ones that have been gently getting you to think about the relationships in your life that are causing you to question if gaslighting is what is occurring or not.

It should be noted, however, that just like all of us, our safe people are people as well; meaning that they will make mistakes, and should be allowed to make them.

They are not perfect, and will often strive to help you to the best of their ability, but that ability may be limited by knowledge, age, or any combination.

If your safe person has, for whatever reason, made you feel unsafe, take a moment to yourself and think about why you now feel unsafe. If you think that this person is actually the cause of the gaslighting in your life, then find another confidant. However, if they now feel unsafe for a misstep with you, such as poor wording or not understanding, think about the conflict and if you feel secure enough, approach them and try to resolve it. Safe people are hard to come by, and they, like us, deserve a second chance if they have proven it.

Boundaries

If you are deep into the personal psychological space, boundaries may be a relatively familiar concept to you, but they will be gone over briefly just in case. As written succinctly in the description of his much more detailed video on boundaries, Dr. Henry Cloud defines the term (2019):

> Personal boundaries allow you to have ownership over your own thoughts, feelings, actions and reactions, while freeing you from being responsible for anyone else's. Virtually

everyone sets some form of boundaries without thinking about it, but when we consciously define them, we gain a huge degree of control over our happiness, comfort and the quality of our relationships.

What this means is that in everyone's life, the boundaries that they have in place are lines that they will not allow others to cross. They could be ethical, what you will or will not tolerate in any type of relationship, or what you as a person are even willing to work towards or not. In relation to gaslighters, boundaries are a huge deal, and can often be a safeguard against gaslighters making you their victim.

If you are unsure if you understand boundaries fully, take a moment to look up what they look like (Dr. Henry Cloud is a great resource for this), or, if you are unsure of your own boundaries, take a moment to think about what they could be. Knowing and enforcing them will become one of your greatest strengths.

Your Brain on Trauma

When you experience trauma, three parts of your brain are affected: the prefrontal cortex (the thinking center) which is under-activated, the anterior cingulate cortex (the emotional regulation center) which is under-activated, and the amygdala (the fear center) which is overactivated (Sweeton, 2017). What this means is that over time, your brain is overstimulated in all the wrong ways, and not stimulated enough in ways that it needs to be. Therefore, making decisions, being able to think clearly, or concentrating could be examples of regular brain activities that trauma victims would find difficult, while other actions like being able to regulate emotions, would be overstimulated and could begin to create over-the-top responses to simple triggers, like experiencing an extreme heart rate in response to a simple prank (Sweeton, 2017).

The Discomfort Zone

The discomfort zone is something that probably only a few of you are experiencing, but it is something to briefly discuss anyways. Essentially, the discomfort zone is a signal in our body that tells us something is wrong through physical or mental stress (Leaf, 2019). It is the over and under reactions in certain parts of our brain, which in normal scenarios, would be reversed (Sweeton, 2017). Over long periods of time, the discomfort zone can actually grow into a form of 'comfort' to people, because their brains have become so adept at handling those types of scenarios, the lack of those feelings would feel unnatural and uncomfortable (Penn State, 2019). People who suffer from long-term gaslighting will often experience these types of brain reversals, since they have subconsciously adapted to always being under either overt or subversive stress.

However, there are many times the discomfort zone is used as a form of inspiration. Consider extreme athletes, thrill seekers, or even business owners. These types of people thrive on the adrenal rush the discomfort zone brings, and use it as a form of battle with themselves to conquer the fear and impossibilities of certain situations.

If you are noticing any of the symptoms of a discomfort zone, or the reversal of your brain in certain stressful situations, begin to actively take note of the surrounding scenario when that happens. Is it because you put yourself in a challenging environment to fight fears or challenge your physical or intellectual prowess? Or is it because you are being pulled into that scenario by someone else?

Journaling

If you are reading this book there is a high chance that

you are looking to validate what is, or has, happened to you; and even if that is not the reason, the following piece of advice is still applicable.

As you read this book, have a piece of paper, journal, or even computer/tablet/phone with you. Something to allow you to stop, think, journal, and really get your thoughts in succinct columns so that you can understand and decipher your own personal scenarios. This book was written with the intent to help you through your trauma and to get past it, but there is only so much a book can do. For each chapter or segment, you will need time to sit and think. Think about what has happened to you, what you noticed, how you feel.

Journaling will be a key component in helping you regain your sense of narrative again, if you have or are being gaslighted. Additionally, journaling throughout this process will help you gain new insights, perspectives, as well as give you good things to talk about with your safe person or a therapist.

If you are living with someone who you believe is your gaslighter, make sure that this journal and book are not in plain view of that person and cannot be easily accessed by them. While this book is meant to help you heal, it could also get a bit messy down the road, so making sure your ducks are in a row without alerting the person who is doing this to you, is the best way to go.

Chapter 1

Understanding Gaslighting

The term 'gaslighting' has become a key buzzword lately, but what does it actually mean? What does it look like? Better yet, how can you recognize it, solve it, heal from it, and potentially avoid it in the future?

In this chapter, we will begin by discussing gaslighting itself. We will discuss the definition of gaslighting, how it works and why it was able to sneak into your life, as well as the 'why' behind gaslighting. Hopefully, by the end of this chapter, you will have a better grasp of what gaslighting is and have a general idea of what it looks like.

As mentioned, if at all possible, have a notebook, paper, tablet, computer, phone, etc., handy for the rest of these chapters. Allow yourself the space to stop and think about what you have read, how it corresponds to your own life, and journal out any emotions, questions, etc., you have. Being able to notice your own thoughts and perceptions as you read will solidify any qualms you have about whether you are being gaslighted or not.

The Actual Term

According to "Very Well Mind" gaslighting refers to a type of emotional abuse where the victim/abusee has their sense of narrative confused to the point where they are unable to make clear, concise judgments about the reality of their situation or even life. The end result is that the victim begins to feel unsure about themselves and their ability to understand the world around them; and it could even go so far as to cause the victim to believe that the majority of the abuse they have suffered is actually their fault, or that it is not really happening (Gordon, 2022).

What that breaks down too is that gaslighting is a form of manipulation where the gaslighter will use belittling and demeaning techniques to cause their victim to doubt their ability to understand, question, or make concise judgments or actions towards their own situations. Every action and technique used by the gaslighter will ensure that their victim will ultimately have no control over their own perceptions of reality.

Gaslighting vs. Manipulation

Since gaslighting is a form of manipulation, differentiating between the two can be a struggle at times. However, a good way to look at it is to attempt to study manipulative and/or gaslighting techniques with the potential end goal in mind.

If the end goal, or result, of the manipulation is that the other person will have ultimate control, then that person is using manipulation to gaslight you (Gillihan, 2018).

Trying to understand or determine the end goal of manipulative actions while they are occurring is difficult at the best of times, but a good way to set the groundwork for figuring out if you are being manipulated or gaslighted while in that moment is to split the two definitions down the fine line that separates the two.

For example, when you are analyzing a scenario either in the moment, or just after, try to determine if you were being manipulated into doing something, versus if your emotions, feelings, and perceptions of reality were being questioned. Consider the following questions:

Am I being manipulated? If so, am I being manipulated into doing something I do not want to do, or into questioning my thoughts, feelings, and reality?

Sometimes we never quite know if we are being manipulated. If you are unsure at the moment, do your best to record the instance and dialogue of what has happened, and go to a trusted third party to gain their insight. They will help guide you.

Additionally, once you have written down the circumstances and dialogue, begin to think about your own feelings. Do you feel confident in your perception of what happened? Was your reality or emotions questioned or belittled at any point in the dialogue?

These are just a few beginning questions to help orientate the difference between manipulation and gaslighting. More in-depth questions, stages, signs, and scenarios will be discussed throughout the rest of the book.

So what does gaslighting look like? Before delving into the specifics of what gaslighting does, how it manifests, and how to avoid or help those causes, it might be useful to see an example.

An Example…

Let's for a moment pretend you have a close friend named Amy, who has been in a steady relationship for the past nine months. This partner is someone you are not super fond of, but so far no glaring red flags have occurred, so you have not confronted Amy about them yet. One night at a party, you overhear Amy's partner saying, "that's not what happened, you need to get over it." While those words are eating at you, you decide that this is neither the time nor place to say anything, so you make a mental note and continue on with your night. A few days later, Amy and her partner have a big argument, which causes her to call you in tears as she explains how that partner was not listening to her needs, was pushing her needs back onto her, and how Amy did not even remember why some of these issues were important to her. Now in a frustrated panic, you begin to make your way to Amy's, all the while trying to figure out how much of this "he said/she said" argument is a red flag versus a serious case of bad communication. Halfway to Amy's apartment, she calls you and tells you everything is fine, that she and her partner talked it out and they both agreed that "she was overreacting", and that "things are fine". Turning back to your home, armed with this new information, you begin to formulate a plan to confront Amy about her gaslighting new partner, and how to help her get out of that relationship.

Before going any further, take a moment with your journal/device and think back on a recent argument or instance where you noticed similarities to Amy. Write down the scenario: What happened, what was said (to the best of your ability), dates, and overall timeline. Chances are, like Amy, this fight subtly continued over several days. Try to see if you notice that pattern.

What to Notice

In the above example about Amy there are several things to note here, and each of them will be divided into 'gaslighting' and 'others'.

The first thing to note is that in this example, you never really liked Amy's new partner. In the case of Amy, this yellow flag does pay off, as it confirms your bad feelings during her fight with her partner. However, for the majority of the scenario, the idea that you were not particularly fond of her new partner can go into the 'other' column, because the result of this yellow flag could go either way. As many of us know, it is quite common for friends to not like new significant others right away, but there are many happy instances where this type of yellow flag resolves itself, and the friends and significant others eventually become quite close. For the scenario with Amy, this yellow flag also pays off, as your lack of goodwill towards the significant other allows you to notice something is wrong before Amy.

Small Note

However, before going on to the second point, it should be noted here that if a trusted friend—and safe person—has repeatedly mentioned to you that your partner is someone they do not like, and they have clear-cut examples of why, their concerns should be acknowledged and listened to by you. That does not mean you need to break up with this person, it is merely pointing out that there are many times that partners and friends get off on the wrong foot, but also your friends have most likely known you longer, and are able to see new partners, normally, in a more clear-cut perspective.

Returning to the Amy scenario, the second instance is what her partner says at the party. The statement,

"That's not what happened, you need to get over it," sounds like pretty solid red-flag territory. And in this example, it is. However, one of the biggest problems with gaslighting is that third parties, and even the victims, need the whole picture to accurately pinpoint what is wrong. For instance, if Amy's partner was actually correct—and in the scenario you do not have enough information to tell—this instance has to be something that is a yellow-borderline-red flag. Why? Because you, as the friend, do not have the entire dialogue. True, the statement, "You need to get over it," is textbook gaslighting behavior. But what if Amy was simply pouting over something that happened at the party? Yes, her partner could have been more supportive, understanding—and definitely should have said a different phrase—but they would not be in the wrong then.

When it comes to gaslighting and dialogue, everyone needs to be incredibly careful that the words and context are explicit. That is the only way to be sure the truth is not swayed.

Third and finally, is the night of the fight. Notice how Amy says that, "She and her partner decided she was overreacting"? That right there is a classic sign of a gaslighting scenario. Together, with her partner, Amy decided that her feelings were not valid and did not need to be acknowledged. Some of you are probably wondering why this can be said in complete confidence, while the second example had so many hesitancies tacked onto it. And the answer to it is simply in the timeline. When Amy called, she explicitly said that she did not feel like she was being heard, or that her needs were not being met, and even worse, that those needs were being used against her.

Anytime someone's needs are explicitly not being met, or pushed back onto the person who has stated them, something is wrong and they are most likely being gaslighted. Relationships are all about communication, give and take, and best of all—allowing the other person to be. And this advice is not just for romantic relationships. This goes for healthy parent-child, coworker, friends, even sibling relationships.

Someone's feelings are always valid, because they are feeling them and they have been brought up by some reaction to an action. How they express those feelings, what they do with them, and how you—the receiver— handle them, are where the messiness of emotions comes up. The same is said for you: Your emotions are valid. Being upset, sad, happy, angry, confused— whatever you are feeling—is valid. It is what you did, and why those emotions popped up, that can be an indicator to root problems within yourself, or within that relationship.

However, as will be said multiple times, in multiple ways throughout this book: Just because someone's emotions are valid does not mean that they have the right to harm you in the process. There are plenty of people who are able to healthily express their frustration, anger, fear, or concern, in ways that are not harmful to the person they have those emotions towards.

So, returning to the third point in the Amy scenario: compared to the second instance, where you overheard the tailend of a conversation, in the fight scene, Amy had several moments of clarity and understanding. She knew her needs were not being met, she knew that her partner was explicitly making her needs her problem, and she was calling you for help. Then, within a span of anywhere from ten to thirty minutes, while speaking to her partner, Amy backtracks and calls to tell you everything is fine. Extreme emotions during conflict are normal, and so is finally acknowledging that something is wrong. The problem is when you have acknowledged something is wrong, but then are somehow persuaded that what is wrong is no longer a problem.

Being talked down from an argument by a partner is

normal, if done correctly and for the right reasons. However, in the case of Amy, her partner deliberately talked her back into an unhealthy relationship, and helped convince Amy that her needs—which to date have not been met—were unnecessary. Never, in any relationship, should the other person make your needs unnecessary. They might not be met in that moment (e.g. you want time off and your boss says no because you have no more that month), but your needs need to be acknowledged.

Yet Another Note

Yes, these notes are numerous—and they will continue throughout this book—because, as with emotions and gaslighting in particular, there are concrete examples, and then there will always be side-stories/scenarios where it somehow looks like gaslighting, but is not (that is not what is happening in the Amy scenario). If you are someone reading this book and you have noticed that someone in your life continually talks down your emotions, take a moment to write down those exact instances in your journal. Then have a moment of brutal honesty with yourself and begin to ask some hard questions, like:

Was I explicitly ignoring a healthy boundary that person set?

Were my emotions being disproportionately expressed towards the situation?

Was the expression of my emotions from a different scenario altogether, and I was unaware, and then they all came out at once?

Has that person been communicating with me, but I was unaware, or, not respectful of that communication?

Questions like these are important because it will help ground the conflicts and fights you have had into a place of hindsight and acknowledgement. Because you need to acknowledge yourself before you can acknowledge gaslighting.

The truth? People are gaslit all the time, and it is an unfortunate and traumatic event that needs to be addressed and that victims need to heal from. However, there are also many scenarios where someone thinks they are being gaslighted, but it is truly a case of not understanding emotions, boundaries, wants, needs, or the compromise relationships—any relationship— takes. Romantically, many people are told "treat your king/queen well," and that is true. However, what that statement does not show is the hard work, compromise, and understanding needed by both partners to make that statement work. The same is said for coworkers, friends, family, and even distant acquaintance-based relationships. If someone has higher expectations, but are unwilling to acknowledge the work they themselves also have to contribute, then claim they are the victim of abuse or gaslighting, then it is actually the opposite.

In any relationship, no matter the type, you need to acknowledge your part in the conflict. It could be as simple as you engaged, or that you ignored something that was bothering you hoping that it was a one-off instance. Instead, what is desperately needed here is for you to completely understand that sometimes what is perceived as gaslighting is actually terrible communication and the manifestation of some type of problem.

Now, returning to the scenarios you wrote down, begin to categorize instances like above, and just use 'other' and 'gaslighting'. Take a few moments to then begin to sort out your emotions—journal them out if you have too—before continuing.

The People Who Gaslight

Now that you have a slight inkling on how gaslighting may be present in your life, or in the life of someone you know, it is time to begin pondering the people who would actually do such a thing. Sadly, gaslighters are typically a form of abusers and manipulators, meaning that they can come in a multitude of shapes and forms, including the intrinsic reason of why they are gaslighting someone. Commonly, gaslighters tend to be pathological liars, narcissists, psychopaths, sociopaths, or even someone who is trying to deal with their own trauma (Gordon, 2022). However, unlike other forms of abusers, gaslighters have one scary thing in common: They are somehow able to gain your trust. And when you think about it, that makes sense, as these types of people need you to trust them. They need an opening into your innermost self and psyche, and if they are in a position of trust, authority, or power, they will have that ability. Gaslighting only works if they are in a position to take all power and authority away from you; and this could be in various forms such as: personally, professionally, romantically, financially, etc. (Gaslighting | Psychology Today Canada, n.d.). No matter what life avenue they use, a gaslighter will always ensure that you think less of yourself, more of them, and rely way too much on their input into your life.

What this also means is that there is not one stereotypical type of person who will most commonly be a gaslighter. Not all pathological liars are gaslighters, although the two tend to go hand-in-hand.

How It Works and Why It Is so Subtle

The fact that there are no distinct, immediate ways to identify a gaslighter is one of the reasons it works "so well" and is so subtle within many cultures, relationships, and group environments. There are even times (like in some of the above examples) that what is gaslighting may not even seem to be gaslighting, or vice versa. Gaslighting is insidious and it usually seems to come out of nowhere. It is sneaky, and like water, trickles a little bit in at a time, in such small amounts that even people who are attuned to the beginnings of gaslighting behavior will sometimes ignore the signs.

But, again… why?

Because the beginnings of gaslighting can come from an understandable place. Sometimes gaslighters are able to hide their abuse for years because it is guised as "caring for you", or "wanting to help you". Or, the gaslighter presented so well at first, the victims just cannot believe that that person is actually a gaslighter. As with any form of manipulation and/or abuse, the person doing it will subconsciously or consciously have a plan to ensure they are not caught. This plan will be the use of words, some actions, or even taking advantage of your weaknesses, to make you reliant on the abuser, unable to believe they are so horrible, or even worse, under their power and unable to escape. They will do anything and everything to ensure that you do not catch on—including using the tactic "flattery will get you everywhere".

So can you tell between a gaslighter and someone that truly wants to help you? A great and simple way that could apply to any stage of gaslighting is how you feel at the end of the conversation. Go back to some of the journaled conversations that you have nearby, and ask the following questions:

Are you uplifted, and ready to change/move forward?

Are you certain about where you are going after the conversation?

Is your perspective clear and concise?

Do you have a clear image of where you are going, and how to do it?

Are you happy with your trajectory, or at least feeling comfortable that you can do the things you have discussed with that person?

Did that person own up to their actions if there was a conflict?

Are you happy with yourself?

Please note that for the last question in particular, it really depends on the conversation you had. For instance, if you were asking for help breaking a bad habit, you will probably not feel good with yourself, and that most likely will not be the other person's fault. However, if you ask them simple questions like: how do I look? What do you like about me? etc., and you are not happy with yourself, something is most likely wrong.

These are just a few examples, and more will be given in upcoming chapters, but the key to notice here is that if you answer 'no' to any or all of these questions, you are dealing either with someone who does not know how to counsel or help you, or a gaslighter—perhaps even both.

Some Notes

It is important to note that there are some small areas that can overlap with gaslighting, including: poor communication and a misalignment of perspectives.

There will be times when these two problems may appear to be instances of gaslighting. However, on further inspection, it is possible to see that they may actually not be a form of gaslighting.

Poor Communication

Unfortunately, there will be times when someone is badly communicating to you, which could come off as gaslighting. Since the idea of gaslighting has only become colloquial within the last decade or so (even though as a term it has been around for much longer than that), there is a chance that you may come into contact with people who are simply not aware that old phrases or sayings, are gaslighting indicators. A great way to clarify that, is to ask. Simply asking: "what do you mean", or "could you clarify" or similar, will go a long way in helping you recognize if someone is a gaslighter or not. If they notice their mistake, or are able to rephrase their previous statement in such a way that your feelings are acknowledged, then chances are, you are fine. However, if that person gets more angry, or continues to aggressively dismiss your feelings, then chances are, they are a gaslighter.

Perspective

There are some people who hear a safe person's perspective and then believe that they are now a victim of another form of gaslighting. That is not to say that they may not be right—there are definitely scenarios where safe people can be a gaslighter, and that will be covered in a different chapter.

In this scenario what is being described are people who have the truth shoved right in their face and they refuse to acknowledge it. Instead, they want to continue to believe that they are the victim, and want everyone to help fix their hurt outside of themselves. Even if those people are being gaslit, if they are refusing to help themselves, there is intrinsically not much that can be done. This book deals solely with you recognizing, and fixing yourself—not the gaslighter. While it would be wonderful to round them all up in a room and force them to go through a seminar and massive therapy to change their ways; that is not possible. The only change that can happen will happen in you. Understanding this and gaining this perspective will help you move forward.

Now, take a few moments and return to your journal. Look at what you have written down, what you categorized from the last section, and now look at the above instances. Be honest with yourself and with your interactions.

The 'Why'

Understandably, if you are suffering from gaslighting, you want to understand the 'why' and 'how'. This book is dedicated to the 'how', but the 'why' is a case-by-case explanation. Perhaps the gaslighter is suffering from some sort of complex, or perhaps they simply want to gain power over the group or individual they are gaslighting.

When thinking about the 'why', the mental road forks into numerous possibilities and people can get lost. The 'why' is definitely important, and for many, it will be a key to healing. But going forward, it is important to understand that the 'why' of your gaslighting, will not be the one magical elixir that will fix the entire scenario. Understanding and comprehending the thoughts, emotions, or actions behind an abuser is only a small fragment of the healing journey—and for many, it is the hardest part. It is impossible not because the answers do not exist, but because the answer is often too simple. Recognizing that you have gone through weeks, months, perhaps even years, of trauma to simply hear that they wanted 'power', or they were a pathological liar, or narcissist, could seem like too simple of a statement for such an awful time in your life.

Yet that is the sad truth to it. Yes, the answer varies per abuser/gaslighter, but the simplicity of that answer will be the same. Unless you somehow have gotten into a relationship with a psychopath or sociopath, there will be no greater master plan that centers around you. There will be no elaborate ruse. There will simply be one answer, one character-based answer that most likely stems from their own trauma, character, culture, or background.

Why is This Even Being Discussed?

Because you need to understand that your abuser is a human too. No, not in the way that you need to extend forgiveness right away (although that will be discussed later). But in the way that your abuser, however sick and awful it sounds, is most likely hurting themselves (unless they are a psychopath, sociopath, or narcissist); and unfortunately, hurt people, hurt people. That is the way of the world, and the simplicity of this answer is sometimes too much for people to accept.

But you need to accept it in order to move on.

It's not You

In order to help yourself from the trauma of gaslighting, one of the first things to acknowledge is that it is not you. You did not ask for this, you do not deserve this, you are in no way responsible for their actions.

Did you stay too long in that environment? Maybe. Did you choose that partner, friend, person? Perhaps. Did you accept that job offer? Of course you did. But just because you took an action of good faith in humanity does not justify what has happened to you. That in no way, means that you deserve this. Ever.

The feelings you may be having right now—anger, frustration, sadness, maybe even grief—are perfectly normal and are no indication that something is wrong with you. As will be discussed in a later segment, grieving the relationship you had, or you thought you had, with the person is an important part of healing.

Rounding It All Up

The last few segments may have seemed like a bit of a jumbled hot mess, so let's put it all together before continuing.

Gaslighting is a form of emotional abuse that causes the victims to begin to question their own sense of reality, perception, and understanding of events. The reason gaslighting is so pervasive in our society is twofold: First, because it is such a subtle form of abuse, many times it comes off as not gaslighting at all—or the victim is unsure if they are being gaslighted, and therefore allow those actions to continue (these are two very specific examples, and more will be discussed in later chapters, do not worry). Second, the people who use gaslighting on others are often hurting themselves, and this could be due to a myriad of reasons like: They are narcissists, pathological liars, want power over anyone and everyone, or they themselves are hurting and this is all they know. On top of that, there are a small number of instances where what appears to be gaslighting could merely be poor communication and lack of boundaries.

Understanding your emotions, how they are triggered, why they come up, and how you present them, are key to understanding other people's emotions and their actions. Understanding, empathy, and a little bit of putting yourself into the other person's shoes will go a long way in finding out if you are being gaslit or not. However, as you begin to try and understand yourself—and maybe your gaslighter—it is important to remember that your 'why' will not be a grand explanation or scheme. It will be a simple answer, and you will have to be okay with that; because this book is about healing yourself, not others. On top of that, accepting the simplicity of the 'why' is going to be a crucial step in your ability to move on and heal from the effects of being a gaslighting victim. But no matter who, what, or how, you have been gaslit, understand this: It is not your fault, you did not ask for this, and in no way shape or form, did you ever deserve it.

Journaling

As you may have noticed, journaling is going to be a key aspect to your healing journey. There are very few things that help center one's mind and emotions than by writing it all down. So, armed with the knowledge of what gaslighting is, how it works, one concrete example, and many side notes, take a look at your previous journaled conversations and write any adaptations, conclusions, questions, or thoughts you have.

CHAPTER 2

Stages and Signs of Gaslighting

When it comes to assessing if you are being gaslighted, there are two key components: the stages and the signs. The stages discuss the different tactics and phases that gaslighters will put their victims through. In comparison, the signs discuss ways to tell if you are truly being gaslighted. Think of it as: The stages are the cause, and the signs are the effect.

Subtle vs. Severe

Gaslighting can present itself in various degrees as well,

and sometimes, it stays at one level instead of escalating into another, while other times it continues to progress. Since gaslighting is a form of emotional manipulation, it has a bigger chance of staying stagnant at one stage if the outcome is what the abuser is looking for.

The type of relationship you have will also depend on how far the gaslighter will go. For instance, it is unlikely that a boss will gaslight you to the point where all choices in your life will go through them, since there are very few ways that they could ultimately have that type of control, unless a romantic relationship has occurred (not to say that this could not happen).

Thankfully, since gaslighters come in different shapes and forms, the "ultimate control" they seek, can sometimes be segmented to just that one area of your life. Yes, the results like possible depression and codependency will trickle into other areas of the victims life, but in other relationships the control might not be as severe. Which is a good thing to remember in the next chapter, where we consider the different types of gaslighting relationships.

Stages of Gaslighting

The stages of gaslighting, or the 'cause' are how the gaslighter will begin to break down their victims own sense of perception, self-worth, and ability to understand their own thoughts, desires, and emotions, so that they, the gaslighter, have ultimate control in the relationship. These stages could happen over a short or long period of time, and victims may not experience all of them, or they could experience multiple at once. Unfortunately it really depends on the situation, the people, and the gaslighter (Ni, 2013).

When it comes to looking at these stages and your own circumstances—or those of someone you know—it is important to know that unlike other forms of abuse, these stages could be very quickly linked together, or take years to accumulate. New victims could easily experience all of the stages in one day, or over the course of years.

Lying and Exaggeration

One of the first stages of gaslighting is that victims will end up being caught in the center of lies and exaggerations. They may not even be big ones; as long as the victim is becoming the epicenter of a false negative narrative, the gaslighter has a way in to begin the rest of the stages (Ni, 2013). Now, as adults in a more or less functioning society, this step may seem a little too much like high school or elementary years.

The problem is that this is exactly what happens. In Chapter 1 we discussed the people who gaslight, and that list included pathological liars and narcissists. Something these types of people have in common is that they will have a long history of not being challenged in a group setting;they will often be the people who somehow have most, if not all, of the group authority and respect. Normally that is because they are able to either bully or lie their way into it, but the thing is: You are going against someone who knows how to work a crowd and who has no shame.

Think about it: If someone has been able to lie successfully for their own benefit for long periods of time, it is highly doubtful that they will feel any type of shame or remorse for their past and current actions. There may even be a possibility that they will be reveling in it. On top of that, these people probably have a no (or very low) history of being challenged for their authority over the group narrative. Their arrogance and confidence have successfully shielded them from scrutiny, and it is this very arrogance and confidence that will continue to shield them, as few will feel qualified to stand up and correct them publicly. Either way, what that means is that gaslighters are not able to feel shame for being caught in their lies, meaning that they will lie and exaggerate confidently, to bring about the outcome they want (Gordon, 2022). Even calling them out for being a liar in front of people will rarely do anything. Unlike the majority of us—who normally still feel some type of remorse when we go against our own code of ethics—gaslighters will not feel bad for what they are doing. So do not rely on their innermost 'humanity' or 'goodness' to come through.

On top of being adept at lying, gaslighters will also make sure that their lies will center around the concept of discrediting and invalidating the victim. Phrases like "you are making this up", "you never remember things accurately", etc., are often used in situations where someone is being gaslit (Gordon, 2022; Huizen, 2020). Using such phrases invalidates the victim, while also putting them on the defensive, and simultaneously causing them to begin to slowly accept the seeds of self-doubt (Gordon, 2022; Ni, 2013).

Another way that gaslighters are able to lie and exaggerate in their favor is by shifting blame and/or rewriting history or events to ensure that it is always the victim's fault or problem (Gordon, 2022). For example, say that you are in conflict with a gaslighter, and when you point out the exact moment that they have been denying exists, they will often respond with, "That is not what happened, and you know it." In this instance, the gaslighter is specifically lying, shifting blame, and rewriting history—all at the same time—to muddle your own perception of events and ensure that their narrative is the one that will prevail.

Repetition

This stage mimics psychological warfare or even mind-control techniques, as the lies and discrediting behavior continue over extended periods of time, with the aim of continuing to wear down the victim's belief in themselves (Ni, 2013). Over time, this will begin to create the dynamic where the victim will actually begin to lean on the abuser, as the abuser's narrative has slowly become the accepted and non-challenged one.

Problems When Challenged

Most people who are abusers do so from a place of hurt or a psychological need for control, and when that control is challenged, they then begin to escalate their tactics—or disproportionately respond to the scenario—in order to maintain that control. These problems can occur in various forms, but two of the dominant forms are denial or diversion (Gordon, 2022; Huizen, 2020; Ni, 2013).

Going back to Chapter 1, when it was recommended that you clarify by asking questions for perspective, this would be a great example of understanding. If you ask a question to clarify what has been said, and the person 'answers' by rebounding onto you, diverting the topic, distracting you, or even discrediting what you think you heard—then that person is a gaslighter.

Remember: Gaslighters will do anything to maintain their control over the narrative, including going out on a limb and denying known events or dialogues. Some of you might be thinking, "Well, that cannot possibly happen if someone stands up to them!" Again, remember, it is most likely that no one has stood up to the gaslighter before, and won. If the gaslighter has been able to avoid any type of shame, consequence, or punishment for their ability to twist collective narratives, they will feel no sense of shame, remorse, or guilt for their actions. There is even a slight chance that they actually believe what they are telling others.

A great example of this is seen often in romantic relationships where someone is cheating. When confronted, many cheaters will completely deny their cheating, even though the accuser will often have non-refutable (or so they thought) proof of the act. In this scenario, if the victim has been gaslighted for long enough, they may actually begin to question the proof that they have of their partner's cheating, even if it is irrefutable to friends and family.

Sounds wrong, right? When looking at gaslighters, it is important to remember: They really will have no shame or sense of wrong, because they already crossed that threshold.

Wearing Out the Victim

Like with so many other forms of abuse, exhausting the victim is key in a gaslighting relationship. The victim needs to be so tired and confused about their own perceptions, that they will actually welcome the 'knowledge' or 'stability' the gaslighter will have come to represent to them over time.

Codependency

According to the Merriam-Webster dictionary, 'codependency' refers to:

A psychological condition or a relationship in which a person manifesting low self-esteem and a strong desire for approval has an unhealthy attachment to another, often controlling or manipulative person (such as a person with an addiction to alcohol or drugs). Broadly: dependent on the needs, or relying on the control, of another. (Merriam-Webster, n.d.)

The creation of such a bond clearly aligns with gaslighting because the victim will completely and utterly rely on their abuser for everything and anything; it is at this point that all control has been given to the gaslighter. The abuser now has the utmost authority to grant whatever they wish to the victim, whenever they want (Ni, 2013).

If you haven't experienced it yourself, some of you may be wondering, "How could that even happen?!"

First of all, do not forget that by the time this stage has come up, victims are at the point where they are not sure of themselves mentally, and have most likely undergone continuous attacks of belittling, lying, and being worn out. On top of that, gaslighters also have a few other sneaky sub-tricks up their sleeve, and these two sub-tricks have the ability to create codependency with their prey.

Using Compassionate Words Against You

The first of these is the use of compassionate words against their victim. Remember earlier how it was mentioned that they will do anything to get their victim's trust, including using flattery? Or that they will often sneak into someone's lives because they "just want what is best for you"? That is exactly what is meant here. Often, gaslighters will find encouraging or compassionate phrases, tones, and sub-actions (meaning they will do that action on the surface, but never follow-through the entire way), to gain their victim's trust and make them believe that they are genuinely a good person. Typically the phrases they use here are red flags to anyone outside of the relationship, because the words that are used are in opposition to the actions that have just happened (Gordon, 2022).

For example, say you were at brunch with your friend, let's call him Adam, and his new friend, Brandon. Over brunch you have become increasingly uncomfortable, because Brandon will say and do things that do not align with each other, such as when Brandon uses intensely hurtful sarcasm to undermine Adam's narrative of events at their work, but ends his sarcasm with something to the effect of, "But seriously, bro, you are great at so many things, but the way you're telling the story is totally wrong, were you even paying attention? Let me tell you what really happened."

Sure, on the surface, there are quite a few "side notes" that could occur here, but let's for arguments sake, say that you knew Adam was not one to exaggerate or lie about how things went down, especially when it was a negative event. Therefore, if you know and trust Adam's perception of events, Brandon's actions can be viewed as acts of belittlement, lying, and causing Adam to reconsider his own perception of events—all while using a compassionate phrase of, "Love you bro. I am just telling you how it is," to gain Adam's trust.

If you are now wondering if the person that has been in your mind this entire time is a gaslighter or not, and specifically if they are using compassionate words to win you over, write down the scenario that is in your head and then ask yourself if their words truly align with their actions. Going back to Brandon and Adam's example, it is clear Brandon does not actually have Adam's best interest at heart, and is definitely not "telling it like it is", because he disregarded Adam's perception. When someone is correcting someone's narrative of how things occurred (and let's be honest, we all know someone who does tend to honestly exaggerate for the dramatic effect), they often do it with words or phrases like, "I do not remember it that way," or, "That does not sound like what I know of this person," etc., most people will base their corrections within their own context of knowledge, which allows everyone within that conversation to line up facts with their own knowledge of people and events.

Gaslighters will never give their victims—or their audience—that chance. Their word will be law, and that is simply all there is to it.

Minimizing Thoughts and Feelings

Leading off of the Adam and Brandon example, there is also another subtle gaslighter tactic being thrown into that conversation: The minimization of Adam's thoughts and feelings on the event at work. When someone minimizes your feelings, they are essentially taking away your right to believe in what you feel. Things like "do not overreact", "you're overreacting", or "why are you so sensitive?" are all classic examples of gaslighters who are trying to gain control over your emotions by minimizing them (Gordon, 2022). And yes, those exact phrases are gaslighter indicators.

As has been said before: Your feelings are always valid, they may just be disproportionate, or badly enacted, towards the event or person that has evoked them. However, if there is ever any circumstance where someone belittles you, or makes you feel bad for those thoughts or feelings in a calm and rational manner, that is not okay and something is wrong.

False Hope

Another stage of gaslighting is giving the victim false hope, or letting them believe that they are right, for small and trivial matters, so that there is some kind of perception of 'equality' between the victim and gaslighter. False hope can come in the form of: mild mindfulness, small validations, or superficial kindness (Ni, 2013).

For example, say during a dinner with a friend and their new partner, you hear the partner mention, "See? If you give me another chance, it can be this good again!" In this example, the partner is deliberately giving your friend false hope. Promising that things could be "this good again", is doing two things: First, it is letting you know that the relationship may not have been as good as it was presented to you. Second, the partner is letting you—the third-party not in the relationship—know that they will do whatever they can to get your friend to stay in the relationship.

Conditional Apologies

Similar to false hope, gaslighters are notorious for conditional apologies, which often sound like, "I am sorry you feel that way, but your feelings are not my fault," when confronted about how their actions have affected you.

In this example, the first part wherein they acknowledged your feelings, is a great way to start an apology. The problem comes up with the 'but' and the red flag becomes noticeable with the end phrase, "Your feelings are not my fault." True, how you feel has absolutely nothing to do with the gaslighter, because it is your body and brain that brought up those feelings. However, the gaslighter is not apologizing for the actions that caused your feelings. Yes, on the one hand, at least they acknowledged your feelings. However, if their actions were genuinely not okay and caused stress and trauma to you, they need to not only apologize for your feelings, they need to take accountability for their actions (Moore, 2019).

This stage is essentially a combination of the problems when challenged, lying and exaggerating, as well as turning back the problem onto you: They ignored a valid argument you brought up (denied the challenge you brought to them), lied and exaggerated through avoidance that they even caused a problem, and turned it back onto you by refusing to acknowledge how their actions created your feelings.

Domination and Control

Domination and control are the ultimate goals for a gaslighter, because they will now have unprecedented veto power over whatever relationship they are in where the victim has become so subjugated to them, they will allow any type of behavior.

If you remember the Amy example from the first chapter—where she calls you in a panic after a fight—she is unfortunately well on her way to this particular stage. She has already been giving signs that she is letting her partner use false hope to lull her into the bad decision of staying in a relationship where over time, through the continued use of the gaslighting stages, all power and control will be given to the partner.

A good way to realize you may be in this stage is to look at your life and really ask yourself how much freedom— and confidence—you have in yourself and the situation, to make any type of decision you want.

Take a Breath

All right, that was a lot of information, so take a deep breath and just sit and think. Grab your journal/device and begin to write out your thoughts, feelings, and any parallels you might, or might not have encountered, seen, or experienced.

Do not give up hope if any or all of these signs are in your life. Now that you are aware, you are slowly gaining back the power that you unknowingly had given up.

Signs You Are Being Gaslighted

Unfortunately, being gaslighted is not an easy

experience that simply takes recognition. As the stages have indicated, gaslighting is a long-term and stealthy form of abuse that the victim may not even be fully aware of. Because the main facet of gaslighting is getting the victim to no longer trust their intuition, it is very probable that the victims are more likely blaming themselves or outside reasons for why that relationship is the way it is. On top of that, there is the strong likelihood that many victims have now given up some type of control, however small, to the gaslighter. It could have even been without their knowledge, as the gaslighter might have used compassionate words, or false hope to get that control.

What this means is that simply being aware that you may be in the process of being gaslighted is simply not enough. If you are reading this book and beginning to notice parallels, that is great (kind of), since that means that you are now aware and hopefully will begin to set the groundwork for getting help.

However, if you are reading this for someone in your life, you need to know that long-term victims of gaslighting could develop feelings of depression, addiction, or even suicide (Gordon, 2022).

If you, or someone you know, is experiencing any of these symptoms, it is important to get help right away, and to ensure that it is a professional who does not know your gaslighter. They must be impartial and qualified to not only counsel you on how to handle your situation, but on how to get out and take care of yourself during the separation process.

Going forward, use the stages as the beginning of self-assessment, as well as ways to begin looking at scenarios around you to pick up on gaslighting behavior. Use this segment as a true self-assessment test.

So, in the words of Sherri Gordon (2022) here are the signs that you have been gaslighted:

- You doubt your feelings and reality: You try to convince yourself that the treatment you receive is not that bad or that you are too sensitive.

- You question your judgment and perceptions: You are afraid of speaking up or expressing your emotions. You have learned that sharing your opinion usually makes you feel worse in the end, so you stay silent instead.

- You feel vulnerable and insecure: You often feel like you "walk on eggshells" around your partner, friend, or family member. You also feel on edge and lack self-esteem.

- You feel alone and powerless: You are convinced that everyone around you thinks you are "strange," "crazy," or "unstable," just like the person who is gaslighting you says you are. This makes you feel trapped and isolated.

- You wonder if you are what they say you are: The person who gaslights you says words that make you feel like you are wrong, unintelligent, inadequate, or insane. Sometimes, you even find yourself repeating these statements to yourself.

- You are disappointed in yourself and who you have become: For instance, you feel like you are weak and passive, and that you used to be stronger and more assertive.

- You feel confused: The behavior of the person gaslighting you confuses you, almost as if they are Dr. Jekyll and Mr. Hyde.

- You worry that you are too sensitive: The person minimizes hurtful behaviors or words by saying "I was just joking" or "you need thicker skin."

- You have a sense of impending doom: You feel like something terrible is about to happen when you are around this person. This may include feeling threatened and on edge without knowing why.

- You spend a lot of time apologizing: You feel the need to apologize all the time for what you do or who you are.

- You feel inadequate: You feel like you are never "good enough." You try to live up to the expectations and demands of others, even if they are unreasonable.

- You second-guess yourself: You frequently wonder if you accurately remember the details of past events. You may have even stopped trying to share what you remember for fear that it is wrong.

- You assume others are disappointed in you: You apologize all the time for what you do or who you are, assuming people are let down by you or that you have somehow made a mistake.

- You wonder what's wrong with you: You wonder if there's something fundamentally wrong with you. In other words, you worry that you are not well mentally.

- You struggle to make decisions because you distrust yourself: You would rather allow your partner, friend, or family member to make decisions for you and avoid decision-making altogether. (Gordon, 2022)

Going Forward

Before continuing onto Chapter 3, where we'll break down gaslighting in different relationships, take a moment to look at the above signs and begin to really ask yourself if you are experiencing any or all of these symptoms. If you are, it is strongly encouraged that you seek help, because these symptoms can get worse overtime and develop into the extreme manifestations that were discussed at the beginning of this segment.

Journaling

If you believe you are a victim of gaslighting, again, write down your thoughts, feelings, and perceptions of this chapter into your journal. Now, armed with the information that you or someone you know is being gaslighted,- make sure this journal is somewhere that is normally not found by the gaslighter if you live together. On your own time, away from your abuser, begin to look for help; but make sure that it is done in a very low-key, operative kind of way. Make sure you close internet browser tabs, delete internet history, and ensure that your phone logs and emails are not immediately accessible to your gaslighter.

Find help. Find a therapist or counselor.

CHAPTER 3

Gaslighting in Different Scenarios

When most people think of where gaslighting occurs, the majority of people will think of close interpersonal relationships like family, romantic, or close friends. One of the reasons these are the first three that usually come to mind, is that these are the relationships that normally display gaslighting first, and they are also the relationships where a gaslighter can gain ultimate power. If you were to move to another city, who would you talk to? Most likely your family, partner, and close friends.

However, that does not mean that these relationships are the only one that can exhibit, or include, gaslighters. Gaslighters can be everywhere, but other, more distant relationships, are only being recognized now. Nonetheless, it is important to remember that in any of the following relationships that will be discussed, the goal of the gaslighter will be to gain ultimate control in the setting where your relationship with the gaslighter exists. For those that are close to you, this could include your entire life sphere, but for other, more distant relationships, this control could be over something as small as your lawn or driveway.

Remember two very important things as you read this chapter. First, there is a chance that the gaslighter is doing all of this harm unintentionally, as painful as that may sound. They may be simply following patterns of behavior that they have seen exhibited throughout their own life, and therefore, are unintentional perpetrators of an ugly cycle. That is not an excuse to forgive them, ignore what is happening, or even to cause you to consider giving a second chance. Instead, those insights are merely presented to give you the ability to make your own judgments about the person you are involved with, and perhaps to give some awareness on the 'why' behind their gaslighting. Second, regardless of what type of relationship you may be in with your gaslighter (if at all), it is not your fault.

Romantic Relationships

Because romantic relationships tend to be one of the more well-known areas of gaslighting (unfortunately), it will be the first relationship discussed. Relational gaslighters also tend to be the two extreme forms of gaslighting: they are either so subtle at it that very few people feel that something is wrong, including the victim; or they escalate so quickly that close friends and family become concerned about the relationship.

When it comes to the manifestations of gaslighting in a romantic relationship, there are several ways that victims can engage in dialogues and begin to express that something is wrong.

They Are not Flawless

It is true, none of us are without our faults, but it is an entirely different matter when our significant other continuously brings them up. Your significant other is meant to acknowledge your flaws and still cherish you, not bring them up in your face constantly and needlessly. By constantly bringing up your flaws, and never mentioning their own, your partner is actually beginning to create a discrepancy between the two of you (Ni, 2013). This discrepancy, like the beginnings of the repetition and codependency in the stages of gaslighting, will begin to shake your confidence and give the gaslighter an opening.

If you are beginning to feel worthless, or even question things about yourself that are not flaws, something is wrong.

Another facet to this particular sign is if they are not willing to admit their own flaws, and even become more aggressive or challenging when you bring them up. Now, as a small note: If they become angry when you retaliate for bringing up their own flaws, there is a small chance that that particular reaction could just be human nature. Very few of us do not act well when we are confronted with our flaws in the middle of a conflict, however, if their reaction is disproportionate, more aggressive, or if they begin to blame you, or even cover up their own flaws with excuses, those are all bad signs (Ni, 2013).

Insecure and Uncertain

If you are feeling anxious and unsure of yourself, something is wrong. There is a small possibility that it could be due to bad communication—especially if you and your partner have been avoiding crucially important talks in the relationship—but as a whole, if you are unsure about where you are, who you are in that relationship, or what you are doing in it, there is a problem (Ni, 2013).

Overly Cautious

In this scenario, cautious means that you are afraid to set-off your partner, disrupt the pattern, or even be a nuisance through normal human functions, like telling them you are hungry and want to eat dinner sooner than you had discussed. If your partner responds poorly to these scenarios, it could be due to either lack of communication, poor boundaries, or gaslighting.

A good way to notice if your partner is gaslighting you and making you overly cautious is to begin thinking about why you are overcautious in the relationship. Is it because you are trying to be aware of past trauma for either you or your significant other? Do you as a couple have bad communication? Is your overcautious demeanor due to a bad fight you just had? Or, is your cautious behavior due to poor boundaries? Many of these problems can be discussed and worked through in a healthy couple, even if they have bad communication or poor boundaries. But it cannot be worked through with a gaslighter.

Another way to look at it is if you do not feel safe enough to express yourself fully and freely. No, that does not mean using unfiltered words or statements. What that means is being able to clearly and concisely: disagree with your partner, stand up to your partner, correct your partner, or state your needs/longings/dreams/problems/questions, to your partner (Ni, 2013). A healthy partner—even if they are a bad communicator or lack/are bad at boundaries— will listen to you if you say that you feel scared to express certain things in the relationship. That discussion could even act as a wake-up call for you both to actively fight previous traumas or bad habits. But a gaslighter, as we now know, will use that discussion to turn all of the problems back onto you and deny their part in it.

A great way to determine if this is happening to you is to take a moment and really think about how you feel when you are away from them. Do you feel better, or worse? Do you feel more free to express yourself? This also works for other forms of gaslighting relationships

You Are Hard on Yourself

Yes, we can all be hard on ourselves. That is a sad fact of life. However, if you are becoming more hard on yourself or start rejecting your background (or even your own values) due to problems within yourself that were brought up by your significant other, then there is a problem. For instance, consider the following statement, "My boyfriend says that I cannot be a good worker, because he says that I cannot finish anything at home."

While it may be true that you do not finish things at home, that has nothing to do with your work ethic. It could just mean that your project management, time management, or self-assessment of abilities needs some work, or even that you deeply hate housework. However, in that statement, the boyfriend has perfectly brain-washed the speaker into believing that they are now a bad worker due to their lack of success at home.

Validation and Excuses

This is a classic abuser symptom: You feel like you need the gaslighters validation, and constantly excuse their behavior. It is one thing to break the habit of needing your partner's validation, and even another thing to acknowledge the circumstances that your partner may come from; but it is something else to completely forgive simply due to those circumstances (Ni, 2013). It is never okay for a partner to use their bad circumstances as a reason to treat you horribly, or to make you feel like you are nothing. And it is never okay for you to change yourself to want someone else's love, approval, or affection.

Friendships

Have you ever watched a movie or drama where there was that one friend that you never understood why they were friends with the protagonist? Or looked at past friendships and wondered why you were ever friends with that person?

If either of those scenarios sound familiar, let's go one step further: Did those friendships portray that friend intentionally getting too close to significant others, closer friends, or parents? Did you notice a rise in gossip, lies, and miscommunication about you wherever you went?

If you answered 'yes' to any of those questions, then chances are that friend was actually a gaslighter. Similar to romantic relationships, gaslighters who present themselves in friends, are predominantly looking for a way to dominate and control you, and in this relationship, they will use their personal influence to begin isolating you and cause you to lean on them for social emotional support. Gaslighter friends are arguably just as dangerous as significant others who are gaslighters, because they have intimate knowledge of how to get a hold of, and control, your innermost circle.

For Example

If there is a small chance you are not recognizing any of these types of instances in your own life, consider this example:

Mary and Alexa were recent close friends, but if you asked either of them, they would claim that it, "Felt like they knew each other forever!" When she had met

Alexa, Mary was already in a one-year heavily committed relationship with Matt. Over the next six months, Matt began to notice that more and more of Mary's time was spent with Alexa, and that some of Mary's previous friendships—which he thought were quite close and high priorities—were no longer being pursued or mentioned in his talks with her.

Then, one day, Alexa calls Matt directly, asking him to help her plan a surprise birthday party for Mary. Thinking nothing of it, Matt agrees and the two talk in secret for several weeks to plan this party. During that time, Alexa goes out of her way to tell Matt intricate details about her conversations with Mary, including when the two women talk about him. This unsettles Matt, but he continues on, since the party is in a few days. After the surprise party, Alexa continues to get closer to Matt. The two would have long texting conversations, and even met for coffee to discuss Mary a few times. One time, Alexa did it with the guise that she was "concerned for Mary", and then proceeded to dish out all the details of a work-related incident to Matt which resembled more gossip than relaying facts. During this talk, Alexa made sure that certain key characteristics Matt knew and loved about Mary (such as her work ethic, integrity, and bubbly personality) were under fire.

While all of this is happening, Mary is beginning to notice that Matt will bring up details and conversations she had not told him, and that some of the things he thinks she has done are not true; including the night Alexa got incredibly drunk and hit on all of the waiters on the way home from the restaurant, only to puke in the cab. Instead of correctly identifying Alexa as the culprit, Matt thought it was Mary, and to Mary's frustration, it took a long time to convince him otherwise.

In Hindsight

When considering the relationship between Mary and Alexa, and then each woman's relationship to Matt: there seems to be something going on. On the surface, this looks like the beginnings of a love triangle, or the possibility for the "other woman" to surface; and that may be true.

However, for the purpose of this book, consider the following tactics Alexa used to begin isolating Mary from Matt:

First: Matt was noticing that Alexa and Mary were spending more time together, and that Mary was not spending as much time on other friendships that she had once held as a high priority. Now, to be fair, that can happen in new friendships; the two people just become so excited that they constantly want to see each other. On the surface, or for very short periods of time, that is common and slightly acceptable. However, in this example, the time period of Mary's declining relationships with others was six months. That is no longer just adjusting to a new friendship dynamic; at this point it could almost be considered a takeover.

Second, Alexa goes out of her way to ensure that she has alone time with Matt. Again, to be fair, it was for a surprise birthday party. Many best friend's have gotten in touch with a significant other to plan those types of events. However, what is key to notice here is that Alexa continued that close bond with Matt after the party. She continued to meet with him, chat with him, and talk with him. On top of that, she has begun to tell Matt things that Mary had never shared with him. When it comes to being the "third-wheel", or the "best friend" in a heavily committed relationship, there are very few times when it is considered acceptable to tattle-tale on your friend to their partner. In this example, Alexa was never given one of those specific instances (but a good one would be if Mary had cheated on Matt, or if she was in trouble and was refusing to tell Matt for his own good).

Third, Matt now has a hard time believing Mary's word over Alexa's. If it had been a night where the three of them had gone out, and Matt was the designated driver and therefore would have had a more sober and accurate picture of how the night's events had gone down, him not believing Mary would be one thing. But for him to just take Alexa's word over his committed significant other—who as far as the example has shown, has no history of lying, cheating, or hiding things from Matt—is a big red flag.

At this point, it can almost be completely believed that Alexa has divided and conquered the couple, and is just waiting for the right event to showcase that dilemma.

While it seems far-fetched, or too based in reality television, this type of behavior is classic for a gaslighter that is a friend. In this scenario, Alexa may have convinced herself she was doing it for Mary's own good. Perhaps she did not like Matt, or wanted to prove that Matt was not as loyal as Mary thought. However 'good' her intentions were, Alexa's actions divided the couple, isolated Mary from her previously strong support group, and began to create narratives where Mary's narrative and character were questioned. All of which are classic gaslighter techniques.

In Families

It is hard to believe that gaslighting could happen in families, as it is often the place people believe they are the most safe. However, families are made of people too, and often in these scenarios the gaslighters are continuing systemic problems they themselves had undergone. It could even be guised as "family traits" or "family mentality" or some such.

That does not make gaslighting okay. But it unfortunately is still possible. For this book, the immediate family, and a few close family member relationships will be covered.

Parents

Since gaslighting is about dominance and control, it is sadly quite easy to implement—even unknowingly—into a parent/child relationship. In these types of scenarios, the gaslighting is often done in an incredibly subtle and even unintentional manner.

Parents who gaslight normally do it through the guise that their child cannot control their own lives; and, arguably that is true for certain times in a child's life— like when they are very young, or they have proven they are not responsible enough. The problem is when that control is not relented to the child as they get older, or become more responsible.

Gaslighting parents are one of the most subtle forms of gaslighting, since the stages and signs are often couched in love, trust, or wanting to help and/or support the child. Additionally, the child will have encountered gaslighting for so long, they may even view that type of behavior as normal, and excuse the signs and symptoms of being gaslighted.

Children who have experienced gaslighting from their parents will begin to show it by feeling that they are always incompetent, unable, or unworthy of certain actions or even affection. An example of this type of scenario would be telling a child that the way they remembered something was 'wrong', or that the child is being "too sensitive" in regards to their feelings. There are several other ways that a parent could invoke gaslighting techniques, including: narrative, emotional, and personal.

Narrative

This refers to when the parents directly question or belittle the child's memory of what has happened. In this scenario, parents may even go so far as to try and convince their child that their (the parents) narrative is the correct one (Colino, 2021).

Small note: This does not refer to a situation where the child may actually forget, or are deliberately ignoring certain facts that occurred within that narrative. For instance, if a small child (let's say around the age of three) argue with their parent that they did not, in fact, bite that other child; and yet the other child in question clearly has teeth marks and there are even witnesses to the contrary of the accused biter—the parent changing the child's narrative is not wrong, but how they go about it might be.

Emotional

Similar to other types of gaslighting, this refers to when parents deliberately ignore or belittle their child's emotions over certain scenarios. Parental gaslighters could even go so far as to wrongly teach their children that their emotions are 'wrong' or "do not make sense" to that scenario (Colino, 2021). Again, as a small note: parents do have the very, very tiny right of helping their child recognize if their emotions are proportionate to a triggering event. Throwing a toy when a parent says 'no', for instance, is rarely an okay form of showing their frustration, anger, or sadness at being told 'no'. And it is clearly within the parents right to teach their child how to substitute their action for a better reaction to showcase their emotions.

The problem is when the emotion is completely invalidated or the parent makes the child feel that their emotions have no right to that scenario. Our emotions are always present, and therefore, have a right to be felt in every situation we are in. The key is to recognize if our display of those emotions is acceptable, if those emotions are a true trigger for what is happening, or if they are coming from a different problem altogether. And when we are very young, it is our parents job to help us begin to realize those differences.

Personal

This type of gaslighting is the hardest to notice—and is often not caught until the child has reached adulthood—strictly because of how insidious it is. In personal gaslighting, the parent has caused the child to now question their own sense of self, specifically their ability to trust themselves, and begin to question what they actually know about themselves (Colino, 2021). Parental gaslighters are able to achieve this within their children by constantly questioning their child's choices, while subtly reminding them about their lack of capability in doing so.

Again, there is a fine line between personal gaslighting,

and true gentle reminders by a parental figure. For instance, for a parent to gently remind a child of when a past decision went poorly, and use that as a learning tool for the current decision they face, is not a gaslighting technique.

Consider the following example: Thomas is trying to help his son, Jack, make a good decision. He uses previous times that Jack made a good decision to help encourage his son to take the step forward—but is willing to step in if something goes wrong. He says, "I am sure that you are able to make that decision, Jack, but you can ask me for help if you are unsure of something."

In comparison, when Todd attempts to get his son, Layton, to make a decision, he does not give Layton that option. Instead, Todd ensures that Layton begins to question himself by saying, "Do you really think you are old enough to make that kind of decision?" In this example, Todd is ensuring that Layton begins to question his ability to make decisions.

Yes, there are times when parents do ask that specific question of, "Are you sure you are old enough to do x", but that is often done in with the Socratic method in mind (e.g. trying to remind the child of previous bad decisions and to avoid it before the parent points it out to them). Or, the question is often followed up with deciding if the child is actually old enough to make a decision based on the child's answer. In Todd's scenario, he is not giving Layton the choice to make the decision, but is rather reminding Layton that since he is so young, he is incapable of knowing what he wants or needs.

For the Parents

You know what? Parenting is exhausting. No one has ever denied that, and parenting a tiny child who has many emotions and a little body that is probably unable to properly express or pinpoint its feelings, makes for a very long and exhausting day. But, that in no way means that you as the parent, are allowed to disvalue a child's feelings, narrative, or understanding of what has happened. While a child's vocabulary may be limited, they will still be astute enough to know when their boundaries are being compromised, and if they are in a healthy enough family dynamic, they will tell you.

Your job as the parent, is to help bridge the gap between events, what the child perceives, and the adult lesson of figuring it out together.

For the Children

Now, on the flip side, if you believe you may have been gaslighted by a parent, and are presumably an adult (or at least older than 13), there comes the inexplicable dilemma of what to do.

If you still live at home, your options may be sadly a bit more limited, as you most likely do not have the ability to set firm boundaries that would necessarily be respected by a parent. If this is you, a great way to confront your parents is by finding a trusted, certified third-party (like a therapist) and confront your parents together.

If you are an adult who has moved out and is just realizing the trauma that you have undergone, there are three options. First, you could record specific instances and confront your parents on your own and try to resolve it 'in-house'. Second, you could consult a therapist and together come up with a game plan on how to confront and fix the relationship with your parents. Third, you could still go to a therapist, but then decide to work on ensuring that you do not continue those behaviors within your own life, and find ways to continue seeing your parents, or not.

The joys of being an adult is that the relationship you

have with your parents are now entirely up to you (situation depending). If you want to continue seeing your parents but want it to be healthy, there are plenty of options to make that happen. For instance, you could create hard and firm boundaries of what is or is not acceptable when it comes to how they can function within your life. Even though gaslighters are manipulators and aren't often confronted, parental gaslighters have this interesting phenomenon where they may acknowledge their wrong doings and accept boundaries that you set. For that to happen the circumstance is dependent on two things: First, and most important, is their own character and willingness to be in your life. If they want to be in your life, and you are firm, then they will have little choice but to acknowledge the new rules you have set. Second is that you have to be firm, clear and concise, and consistent in the boundaries you set.

Here is an example from a friend when she was younger (this example is purely on boundaries and has nothing to do with gaslighting, but the correlations will be explained). Whenever this friend misbehaved in a grocery store, her mother would simply and calmly tell her that she had three counts and if, at any time, the friend continued to be incorrigible in the store or belligerent to her mother after the count of three, they would leave. What this means is that this friend had the ability to change her attitude anytime up to her mother saying the word 'three'. If the mother got to three and the child had not changed, they left, end of story. In this example, the friend acted out a total of five times before she learned that her mother was serious about the number 'three', and that while her feelings and emotions were valid, they were not being proportionally, or appropriately, displayed for the setting of the grocery store.

In this example, the friend's mother clearly, succinctly, and consistently followed through with the boundary and an understanding that while in a store, certain acts of decorum were expected. The friend had several instances where she wanted to test that boundary, but her mother did not let her. Similar to my friend, you have to be just as firm with parents who are unintentional gaslighters. Parents that are gaslighters unintentionally often do it out of a misplaced sense of love, duty, or parenting, or, they are continuing a cycle that they themselves endured. Yet if they are teachable and willing, together, you can stop that cycle through the simple use of enacting boundaries.

On the other hand, if you believe that your life cannot be healthy with your parents, then you have to come to grips with the trauma that you have suffered, and find ways to move on. This could apply to someone whose parents do not respect their personal boundaries, intentional gaslighting from the parents, or because too much damage has occurred for someone to consider opening the door just yet.

At this point, whatever you choose is entirely up to you; but it is recommended that you get third party and/or professional help in making those decisions.

Siblings

Similar to parents, having a sibling that is a gaslighter has the potential to be deep-rooted and hard to spot. Siblings who gaslight each other often occur in a similar manner to parents; the abuse and belittling of your emotions and/or narrative, will be guised as love, care, support, or bullying.

While siblings may seem like an easier fix, the instances of their gaslighting may be a bit harder to spot, or to alert someone for help, depending on the circumstance. If you are still living at home, make sure to record any instances of gaslighting and to alert an authority figure within your family or someone who has the ability to help your situation. Whoever you pick has to be able to listen to your problems and confront the gaslighter with you.

If you are an adult who is just coming to realize that your sibling relationships are full of gaslighting instances, similar to the above parental situation, you have three options: you can either confront, confront with help, or get therapy on your own and ignore the relationship.

Authority Figures

Authority figures in familial settings translate to anyone who has the potential to control you while in that setting. It could be a grandparent, aunt, uncle, godparent, etc. When it comes to gaslighting, the signs and stages will be the same, and the desire for control will mimic those that were found in the parent segment: They will want control mostly because it will be best for you, or to maintain the familial status quo of what does or does not happen.

Compared to your parents, these figures may not have as much sway within your close-knit familial unit, depending on the relationship. For instance, if the gaslighter is the family matriarch, they may in fact hold more sway than parents. But if the gaslighter is an aunt, the control they exert over your life will be limited.

These types of gaslighters, just like all familial relationships, can be dealt with in three ways: you can either confront them on your own, armed with sound knowledge, gain help from an outside source and confront them together, or find a way to gain your control back and establish firm and hard boundaries that will negate the ability to be gaslit in the future.

Cousins

Not many of us see our cousins on a daily basis, so that makes seeing them—and knowing they will try to gaslight you—all the more frustrating and difficult. Distant familial relationships often have gaslighting instances continue for longer than they should have, strictly because these relationships are not consistent. It is hard to enforce boundaries, or even notice wrong behavior that is subtle like gaslighting, when you see someone so rarely throughout the year.

That is not an excuse to let bad behavior continue, though. Instead, it just means that these types of relationships may take longer to recognize, change, and/or deal with.

Also, gaslighting in cousins may seem a bit odd, because as a generational peer, how could they possibly gain control over you? In this instance, it may not be control per se that they are seeking, but it is the undermining and making the victim seem not as perfect, or as accomplished, as the rest of the family thinks they are. Most cases of gaslighters who are cousins are misconstrued as manipulation or a form of bullying. In any of the scenarios, the end goal of making you appear to be less than you are, is still valid and needs to be addressed by you in the ways that have been described so far.

Outside Relationships

Outside relationships refers to people that are more like close family friends than blood relatives. These people could be godparents, your 'aunt' or 'uncle' (perhaps not by blood relation), etc.

The gaslighting behavior these relationships would display are no different than any other authority figure that has been discussed so far, however the end goal of ultimate control may be a little bit different than a blood relative.

Unlike older relatives, where authority, control and respect are assumed/automatically given due to the nature of their relationship with you, outside 'familial' authority figures may attempt to use gaslighting in order to compensate or gain the type of control in your life that they do not automatically have.

Even if that is their motivation, the way they go about it is never okay; and even though they are not blood relatives, you still have every right to be upset, annoyed, or frustrated at their actions. The confrontation options are the same for these relationships as all other familial ones.

The Workplace

When it comes to the workplace, there are two predominant types of gaslighters: your boss, and your coworkers. Each scenario and relationship will be discussed so that you have a clear picture of what they can look like. Notes, comments, and examples will then be split up between bosses and coworkers.

Persistent Negative Narrative

If you are wondering if you are being gaslit in the workplace, one of the first questions to ask yourself is if the narrative around you—as a person—is always negative. Have you heard coworkers or bosses say that you are a negative influence, a negative worker, or that you do not shape up to your peers? It is important to note here that when it comes to gaslighting in particular, the negativity you should experience has to be incredibly personal and based on an almost biased perspective from the other person (Ni, 2020). If you hear negativity after a bad performance review—that you deserved—then you are not being gaslit. However, if the accusations, or rumors, you hear are not well-founded, or have no groundings, then there is a problem.

Constant Gossip

Which brings up the second sign: Do you somehow manage to find constant gossip about yourself, or find yourself always tangled into some sort of office gossip chain? Please note that this does not count if you are actively discussing the gossip of your own free will, or perhaps even starting the gossip yourself. This scenario specifically refers to the type of gossiping scenarios that would catch you unaware and completely out of left-field (Ni, 2020).

Negative Comments or Public Image

When looking at this information, it is important to remember that these explanations and scenarios build off of the previous chapters—which means that most of the negative situations that are being used as examples here are with the intent that it is false. A gaslighter will do anything to make you look bad, and that will often be at the price of your personal, professional, and relational integrity; all with the desire of making themselves look good and enforce their own narrative.

Which plays perfectly into negative comments or a bad public image in the workforce. Did you have a spotless record when you first started work, but then have begun to notice its decline and lack of respect towards you, based on unfound comments given by someone in your workplace? In this section, these negative comments would have to be in a public setting, like: office meetings, client meetings, introductions, socials, etc.—anywhere that would give your gaslighter the ability to bad-mouth you in a setting where you are either too helpless, professional, or unaware, to correct the lies (Ni, 2020).

Negative Humor and Sarcasm

The entire concept of the "just kidding" (jk) joke has been around for quite a while, but it is only coming to light now with how harmful those jokes can sometimes be. In fact, 'jk' jokes are sometimes the bread and butter of professional gaslighters, because it gives the signal to others that whatever belittling, mean, hurtful, or incredibly cruel sarcasm they have just used, was all under the guise of a 'joke'. But was it actually a joke? In the use of a gaslighter—no, it was not.

In fact, negative humor and sarcasm is a powerful tool that gaslighters use in the professional space to enforce a gaslighters main tactic: to belittle and dominate their victim (Ni, 2020).

Professional Exclusion

Sometimes this particular tactic can be tricky because while some employees feel that they are being 'excluded' they are in fact, just too junior or not perceptive enough to be included in certain types of meeting. The good news is that many companies and Human Resource workers are working to include programs that will help make this type of exclusion less and less.

The entire reason that little footnote was brought up was to show how gaslighting works with exclusion in the workforce. Typically, professional gaslighting through exclusion can be tacked onto other terms, like the "Good Ol' Boys Network", "The Glass Ceiling", racism, sexism, etc., (Ni, 2020). What that breaks down too is a subtle form of gaslighting which tells someone they are incredibly competent. In fact, competent enough to train someone else—but not competent enough to actually take that position.

Bullying and Unequal Treatment

In terms of professional gaslighting, this can be considered the 'height' of it; as this is most likely how dominating a gaslighter can get in the workforce. Bullying is never okay, and should always be stopped, but what happens when it is your boss? That can become a whole new barrel of fish that many people would rather suck up and take, because they need the job; and fair enough. Getting and keeping a job can be tough sometimes. However, if your boss begins to make you feel less than, and uses phrases like, "No one else will hire you," or, "You are incredibly unqualified and yet I still hired you," or anything to make you feel like you do not deserve the job you have and should worship the ground they walk on—they are not only a bully, they are a gaslighter.

Instead of bullying, the gaslighter may instead give them subtle unequal treatment within their team or department. These little things could be numerous, but result in the victim feeling like they do not belong on their team, or that they may not even deserve to be there; even though their qualifications, merits, work ethic, and everything else, says otherwise.

When it comes to gaslighting in the workplace, the signs and stages are the same, but how they are used depends on who is gaslighting you.

Your Boss

For instance, when it comes to your boss, certain gaslighting behavior may be more forgivable for a myriad of reasons. Perhaps they are bad at communication, perhaps they pay you too well to quit, perhaps you feel indebted to them, or perhaps there is a large generational gap that many of these problems are being blamed on.

Regardless of circumstance, the biggest problem with gaslighting bosses is that they already hold all the power.

They are the final (or next to final) say. These are the people who can fire you at a moment's notice, without much scrutiny. It makes sense that you, as the victim (or someone you know), are unwilling to disrupt the entire company for one boss. Yet, let's look at it another way: There is a strong chance that you are not the only employee that is being gaslighted, or that this has happened before; especially if the boss is older. Do you really want to keep your head down and let someone else suffer?

Please note: This is not a certifiable letter of approval to immediately quit your job. Your friends, family, maybe even coworkers or team members, would know better. This is instead a wake-up call that if you are using any of the above excuses and still feel or experience any of the previously mentioned circumstances or feelings; something is wrong, and it needs to be addressed.

An Example

Before moving on to coworkers and gaslighting, here is an example of how a boss could gaslight an employee:

Travis has been working at a new office job for several months, but has noticed that the boss for their department is a bit of a tough older gentleman. The way he speaks to employees could be considered a "generational gap" in political correctness, or even sensitivity, and for the most part, Travis is able to ignore it. However, this boss has started to make comments to Travis similar to, "I could get many other people to do this job," or, "I am not sure that your job is entitled to as much pay and resources that it gets, how do you intend on making sure you are worth what we pay you?" As time goes on, these comments towards Travis become more consistent and hostile, and friends and family have noticed that Travis is not as happy as he once was, and has begun to dread going to work more than any other previous position.

Notice how in the above example, Travis explains away a lot of his boss' behavior as a systemic problem of generational gap, or lack of sensitivity. Which is understandable to identify and acknowledge. The problem is that Travis allows this behavior to justify certain treatments he himself is being subjected to. Belittling Travis by saying that anyone else could do this job—regardless of the experience and qualifications Travis has—is never something that a boss should say to an employee. This may be said behind closed doors to Human Resources when discussing an employee's pay or circumstance, but saying it to Travis was unacceptable.

Additionally, the boss has begun to make Travis question his overall worth and what he brings to the company, by constantly telling him to ensure that he is worth the money the company pays him.

When a company hires you, it is with the understanding that you are worth whatever your yearly salary is, and that the job requirements will fulfill that worth combined with your expertise. Unless they have been promoted, or there are explicit requirements that are not being met (such as bad work ethic, or a misunderstanding of job duties), an employee should never have to justify to an employer how much they are worth once they have the job (negotiating is common when obtaining a job, and that is an entirely different scenario).

At the end of the day, unless you have been fired, your boss never has the right to make you feel like you do not deserve your job or that you are unqualified. They do have the right to point out where things are wrong, where you could improve, or what you need to change; but that always has to be said in a respectful manner. Making you feel like you do not deserve to be there is inappropriate.

If you believe that your boss is gaslighting you, reach out to Human Resources with proof of the gaslighting (either recordings, emails, etc.), and follow company protocol on how to handle the situation.

Your Coworkers

When it comes to your coworkers, your company should have built-in systems for team disagreements and conflict resolutions. The key here is to begin documenting the instances where you feel that you are being gaslighted, so that when you confront the gaslighter either with your boss or Human Resources, it does not become your word against theirs. Remember: Every gaslighter makes sure that they control the narrative, and your coworker will be no exception.

The types of gaslighting coworkers will employ center mostly around ensuring that your narrative of events is never believed by the rest of the team/floor/cohort. Tactics like gossiping, lying, exaggerating, etc., will be predominantly used in these types of scenarios.

For coworker relationships it is important to remember the discussion in earlier chapters about how gaslighters have confidence and lack of shame when it comes to their actions. Confronting them in front of the rest of the team/company/cohort will not do any good, as they will not feel shame.

Instead, confronting them with solid proof and an authority figure who will be able to enforce healthy boundaries and put certain protocols in place to protect you and the situation, are the best way to handle coworker gaslighters.

Safe People

Ironic, right? The very reason they are called 'safe' people is so that you are able to avoid the types of scenarios where they would harm you. The problem is that gaslighters can be everywhere, including the ones you confide in. In actuality, being a safe person for their victim is one of the dream spots for a gaslighter, as they will have a lot of control over your life and be able to regularly employ the concept of fake compassion, caring, or sympathy, to ensure you do what they want. Now, as a small note (and as was discussed in the Introduction), there is a small possibility that your safe person is actually safe, and just needs to update their jargon or understanding of how emotions work (e.g. if there is a generational or cultural gap, or communication error, etc.). So if you are curious if your safe person is actually safe or a gaslighter, pay attention to their words, the stages and signs, and your emotions during your interactions with them.

Thankfully, the signs, stages, and tactics for spotting gaslighters are the same for safe people as it is for anyone else. The problem is getting you to recognize and pinpoint that it is your safe person that might be getting you to feel that way.

Again, asking questions that identify how you feel about yourself will be key in recognizing if you are being gaslighted, or if something else is happening.

These questions could be something like:

Was my narrative questioned to the point where I feel belittled, dismissed, or disregarded? Some safe people want to ensure that the dialogue is what you say it is before they give their advice. That is not gaslighting behavior, if anything, that is protection for you. If a safe person gave advice off of a dialogue that you are not sure about, they may make the situation worse. For a gaslighter to surface, they have to be saying things like: "that is not what happened". You need to feel that your narrative was being questioned to the point of disregard, belittling, or dismissed.

Did they belittle how I felt? A key point of safe people is to validate your emotions in ways that allow your emotions to exist, while also being open to the option that you may have missed some key elements to the scenario. For instance, it is very common for a safe person who is a friend to validate your feelings, while also gently reminding you that the person you are in conflict with could have a good reason behind their actions. However, if they say something like, "You are overreacting," or, "Your emotions do not suit this scenario," etc., then something is wrong.

Neighbors

First of all, some of you may be wondering if it is even possible for your neighbors to gaslight you; and to a point, that is a valid question. At most your neighbors are a type of friend, and therefore the type of gaslighting they could use on you would fall more into the friendship category. At the very least you share some grass, maybe a driveway or a wall with them. How could such little contact create gaslighting?

Quite simple, actually. Since your interaction with the neighbors could be as benign as a simple 'hello' or acknowledgement that they are home, they are able to gaslight you quite easily because you are never entirely sure of who they are as a person, or what they are doing. This form of gaslighting is so obvious that it takes a lot of people by surprise: denial.

Consider some of your most recent interactions with your neighbor that involved confrontation. Did the neighbor flat out deny that it happened? Or round the questions back onto you? That right there is pure, unfiltered gaslighting.

For example: You confront your neighbor John about the fact that the tiny piece of grass between your house and his, has grubs in it. You can clearly see the circular brown spots, and your night cameras have picked up the skunks and other critters digging up the lawn to eat them. Normally, this would not have really done anything to you, but since you are concerned the grubs could pass over onto your other lawn, you decide to confront John about it. However, when you tell John that there are grubs, and you have even dug one up for evidence, John simply denies it by saying, "Well, I do not know where you got that little guy from, but it is not from the piece of lawn between our houses. You are clearly making this up and are mistaken."

To anyone—even someone who is unfamiliar with noticing gaslighting—that entire conversation was accusatory and deliberately ignorant of the facts. Which, as you now know, are common signs of being gaslighted.

Sometimes gaslighting is actually blatantly in front of us, and we are either not certain, or clearly astounded by the audacity someone could have. But it is possible.

Confronting a neighbor is the best way to confirm if they are a gaslighter and to begin figuring out if there is a way that you can solve the situation peacefully. If the neighbor, like John, seems to be unwilling to find a compromise or attempt to fix the problem, then higher authorities—like the landlord or bylaw—should be contacted with the proof that you have gathered.

Other Professions

It is a sad fact, but there are many people—women in particular—who are gaslighted by other professions, especially in medicine. History is chock-full of these types of examples, from women being sent to insane asylums for simple socially unaccepted problems (like libido, depression postpartum, etc.) or even modern day women being told what they can or cannot do with their reproductive organs (Moore, 2021).

However, those specific tirades will not be discussed here. They are simply being mentioned to point out that professions have a history of gaslighting those they feel they can take advantage of; and unfortunately the medical field is one of the top fields where this practice is still common. Similarly to the neighbor scenario, gaslighting in other professions is usually blatantly obvious. Victims just do not want to recognize or acknowledge that they have been gaslighted, either because it would be more work to find a replacement professional, they are surprised, they are taken aback, or they somehow believe the gaslighter.

Fixing professional gaslighting is actually quite easy: You simply find a new professional, and take documented evidence to authority figures (like the owners of the firm or clinic, or to ethics boards).

Summing it All Up

Again, that was a lot of information to go through, so first of all, grab a cup of tea or coffee and just sit and let your thoughts percolate for a few minutes. Then, grab your journal and begin to write out which relationships you have been noticing the signs and stages from the previous chapter, or the types of similarities you noticed in the examples that were given.

Take a moment to really sit and think, and allow yourself to feel the emotions that those thoughts bring up. If you are a victim of gaslighting, you probably have not felt like your emotions were valid or okay to be expressed for a long time; and it is time to change that. You are allowed to be upset, to be angry, and to be hurt and angry with the people that have done this.

Whichever relationship you have identified your gaslighter to belong, remember: None of this is your fault.

CHAPTER 4

Dealing with and Recovering from Gaslighting

Now that gaslighting has been identified, broken down, and some of the possible relationships/examples have been given, it is time to begin discussing how to deal with the gaslighters in your life and to begin the road to recovery from those experiences.

Dealing with Your Gaslighting Experience

Dealing with your gaslighting experience refers to the

simple acknowledgement that you are being gaslighted, and then following prescribed steps to help begin to separate yourself from the situation.

Write down the experiences where you believe you are being gaslighted and to ask a third party, preferably someone experienced like a therapist, for their opinion.

So how do you go about that? Sherri Gordon has several ideas::

First, gain some distance from your gaslighter (Gordon, 2022). Even if they are your spouse, find a way to spend a few days with someone you trust. During that time, use the space you have gained to begin putting perspective onto your situation. That could involve coming to face some hard truths, like you allowing certain behaviors, or not standing up sooner. All of those types of emotions are okay, just ensure that you feel those in a safe space and to not consult or talk to your gaslighter while you are feeling those emotions. If you are unable to physically leave the space, then begin to take up practices like meditation, deep breathing, and grounding exercises.

Second, begin to record evidence (Gordon, 2022). This could take the form of voice memos, screen shots, the journal that you have been using throughout this book, and/or saving texts or emails of situations where you believe you are being gaslighted . When saving the evidence, ensure that it is saved somewhere that your gaslighter is unaware of, and is in a place they do not have easy access too. Additionally, make sure that they are unaware they are being saved or recorded. If the messaging app you use with that partner has a notification for when a screenshot of the conversation has been taken, find a disposable camera and take pictures of the conversation that way. While it is not encouraged to hide information like that from the people you love, if the people you love are hurting you, then you have to put your own mental and emotional safety first. Same applies to other relationships like with a boss or coworker—always save the evidence somewhere they cannot find it and in a way where they remain unaware of your actions.

Third, set boundaries (Gordon, 2022). This has been discussed in the introduction and previous chapter, but as a reminder: A boundary is telling others what you are willing to accept in a relationship. So when you are being gaslighted by someone, saying something along the lines of, "I do not accept that type of language used around/about me," or, "I do not accept when lies are being told about me,". These statements will put the gaslighter on notice that you are no longer going to stand for their game. But be careful, this will also mean that your influx of evidence may begin to slow down, especially if they listen. However, if your gaslighter listens based on your verbally setting boundaries, that is actually a great sign. If the gaslighter does not respect your boundaries, it is now up to you to enforce them. Enforcing your boundaries could be a simple reminder to leaving the scenario entirely; including leaving a restaurant, your home, etc. If you need to go to those levels of extremes, make sure that you have a third party on standby, or money on hand, so that you have somewhere safe to go.

Fourth, get an outside perspective (Gordon, 2022). As has been mentioned constantly so far, an outside perspective will go a long way in helping you recognize your disorganized, or unclear, emotions and their relationship to the scenario. Not only will an outside perspective help you figure out your emotions, they will also provide the validation you need if you are being gaslighted.

Fifth, end the relationship (Gordon, 2022). This applies to any form of gaslighting, including professional or familial relationships. At the end of the day, gaslighting is a form of abuse, and any relationship that perpetuates abuse is not one that you should stay in. Even if it is your significant other, parents, or boss.

Now, how you end the relationship—or how to deal with ending that relationship—will vary depending on what the relationship was. Ending a familial relationship will most likely be painful, hurtful, and possibly even more traumatic than a bad ending to a romantic relationship, because compared to a significant other, your family are the ones who are meant to protect you and always be by your side. However, if anyone in your family is abusing you—and remember, gaslighting is abuse—then you have to end it. Would you encourage a friend to stay in a physically abusive relationship with their parents, siblings, aunts, uncles, or boss? No? Well then, why would you encourage them to stay in an emotionally abusive relationship with any of those people?

It May not Be Forever

Compared to other forms of abuse, there is a chance that your gaslighter is doing it unintentionally; and that they may change once their behavior has been broken down and taught as to what they are doing, why it is unacceptable, and how to change that behavior. That change starts with you. It starts with you confronting the gaslighter with your evidence and possibly introducing a third-party to help explain why you feel the way you feel, why you are leaving, and how their actions have helped cause this problem to go this route.

However, there is no guarantee that the gaslighter will want to change, can change, or that you should be there for that journey. Going back to an extreme example: Would you encourage your friend to stay in a physically abusive relationship while that partner went into intense counseling? The same applies to gaslighting victims. They/you are in no way obligated to stay and help their/your abuser along that journey, even if they are your parents, spouse, friend, colleague, mentor, etc.

Recovering

In comparison to dealing with gaslighting, recovering from your gaslighting experience is going to be a longer and more intense journey. Partly because this period of gaslighting has to deal only with you: How you are going to deal with the trauma of your experience, how you are going to ensure that your recovery continues, and how you are going to put yourself into a better place going forward.

Good news is that these topics will be discussed in this book and in the following sections. But it is important to reiterate: While the steps and helpful points can be shared, it is up to you to now do the hard work.

What Recovery Looks Like

Recovering from gaslighting is going to take some time. Like with any type of trauma, your emotions, sense of self, and honestly—just your entire being—need to rest and find ways to begin living again. This section will predominantly deal with ways that you can begin to recover, but remember: Most of this segment is general guidelines. For true and personalized recovery, ask a professional.

So, without further ado, here are a few generalized ways to begin your recovery:

Get Your Own Space or Get Your Space Back

As has been stated before, space is a great way to get emotional distance from your gaslighter. However, compared to the previous section, this space is moreso referring to a clean slate.

For instance: Get a new apartment (if possible), get a new job, go back to older, more healthier friendships, remove yourself from that social circle entirely. How your clean slate state is going to look will depend entirely on the relationship you had with your gaslighter, but this is a crucial first step in beginning your road to recovery.

Gaining a new, safe, and non-toxic space will allow any emotional attachments you created to your gaslighter through previous surroundings or people to no longer have any sway on your decisions, or future emotional phases. Additionally, a new space will help you make an entire safe place to process the trauma you have experienced.

One important aspect of this new clean slate is to completely stop contact with your gaslighter (Sarkis, 2019). Yes, the previous section did have that footnote about how stopping contact may not be forever. But realistically, there is a very small percentage that that scenario will happen; and you need to be okay with that. Whoever your gaslighter was, they had ensured that a portion or all of your life included them in some way or another. Now is the time to stop that, to build your life for yourself, and to begin to remember what it felt like to be independent without that person. Even if it is a family member. Truthfully, this step is probably going to be the longest and hardest, because your gaslighter had become a big portion of your life, and you are intrinsically cutting off a part of your life that you had been reliant on for probably a decent amount of time—even if that part of your life was toxic.

It is imperative that during this step you do everything in your power to maintain healthy relationships with those around you who are supporting you throughout this journey. They could be friends, therapists, family members, even a pet, because cutting out the gaslighter is going to feel like there is a big hole in your life, and the goal of this phase is to ensure that you do not find another toxic relationship to fill it.

You Might not Get Closure

Remember in Chapter 1 when the 'why' was discussed? That segment was brought up early on to begin setting the groundwork for this particular section: the closure you feel you need, and are entitled to. Closure, confrontation, revenge, justice—whatever label you want to give it—there is a big chance that either you, or someone who is on this journey with you, wants your gaslighter to pay. And that payment often needs to come in the form of an in-person confrontation.

Let's save you a bunch of heartache and extra therapy

sessions. Do not do it. You may want too, the need to do so is probably burning a hole in your gut just reading this section. But here is the thing: Whether your gaslighter was a narcissist, pathological liar, sociopath, or just plain misinformed and unintentional in how they hurt you; engaging is not always going to help.

If your gaslighter has not yet had their acceptance moment which has ignited their will to change, talking to them is going to do absolutely nothing (Sarkis, 2019). In fact, it may be even more harmful, because that final talk will give them the ability to turn everything back onto you (remember, this is a gaslighter we are dealing with).

So save yourself some energy, time, and extra hurt. Do not do it.

Grieve

This step may seem a little odd, since you are getting rid of something that was toxic to you. However, it is completely normal and natural to grieve the loss of that relationship, job, or situation. The sadness you are feeling is not because you lost something good, it is most likely because you are mourning the time you lost in that situation, the choices you made, or how you lost yourself; and that mourning needs to happen. You need to grieve what has happened to you to begin the journey of validating your own emotions again. Just ensure that this phase includes safe people or your therapist, as they will help ensure that you are grieving healthy things, instead of the lack of toxicity you are now experiencing.

That Sounds Weird

Weird, right? Why would you mourn something that was toxic to you? Because there is a good likelihood that that toxicity was all you knew for a long time. That is even more true if your gaslighter was a family member, close friend, or significant other.

Grieving and going through those steps is a way to begin to remind your body and brain that it is time to actually move on. When it comes to gaslighting, or any type of trauma, you will not only be grieving whatever loss you are feeling, your body and brain will also be 'grieving' the lack of trauma it has become accustomed to. Even though this is a healthy step and something you need to do to recover, your body will still be in a bit of a whirlwind on how to adjust to the lack of trauma, depression, confusion, or isolation it has been subjected to for the duration of the relationship with your gaslighter.

This includes your brain, which handles essentially every

part of this process. Remember the section in the Introduction called 'Your Brain on Trauma'? That leads us here: The grief you are experiencing is also your brain and body's way of recognizing that how it has previously handled emotions and stressful situations will no longer be necessary, and it is quite possible that a lot of pent-up emotions will now be released with no real reason, other than your body needs to process it all (Sweeton, 2017). Essentially, you are foregoing the Discomfort Zone for the Comfort Zone of the brain, and that transition will take time and many emotions.

In most cases, the grief you feel is not just over the actual relationship, the time lost, or what has happened to you, it is also your body's way of reacting to the loss of a presence that you had believed was going to be comfortable to you. Think of it like a massage, chiropractic adjustment, or even yoga after a bad day: Your body needs to physically, mentally, and emotionally, release the negativity it has been holding onto. And you need to let it.

Reconnect and Volunteer

Part of the grieving process is reminding yourself that you are part of the living, and two ways to do this are through volunteering and reconnecting with people you had fond memories with or were close to before your gaslighter entered your life (Sarkis, 2019). Reconnecting with those you were close to in the wake of recovering from gaslighting makes perfect sense, as you were most likely isolated either by your gaslighter or emotional repercussions. Once again being in contact with people who were positive will help you remember the good times before the gaslighting, and will hopefully give you enough incentive to seek out more positive relationships going forward.

But what about volunteering? There is something therapeutic about volunteering for other people, because it will do two things; first, it will help you remember that you have value and can help others, even when you are broken or hurting yourself (Sarkis, 2019). Secondly, volunteering will help to fill the void in your life that the absence of your gaslighter will have caused (Sarkis, 2019). Sometimes there is truly nothing better for an idle or grieving mind than busy-ness.

However, please note that you cannot use volunteering as a way to avoid recovering or avoid facing hard truths about your circumstances. Many people, unfortunately, use volunteering as a way of therapy, and that is not the point. It is encouraged to volunteer to help you get out of your head and to give your brain something to focus on other than your own negative circumstances, or the lingering effects of it. Not to completely substitute one situation for another.

Focus on Yourself

Recovery is a time to be all about yourself. Not in the way that the world revolves around you, or that you should become that person who will butt ahead in line because you "just need that last muffin" at the coffee shop. In order to recover, focusing on yourself means that you will become attentive to what you need in the present to maintain your new-found sense of 'self'. You need to prioritize self care, your emotions, and being able to admit that you have made mistakes.

Essentially you need to focus on recognizing all the signals your brain used to have (or could have) before the gaslighter came along. When your brain tells you you need alone time to focus on yourself, or to feel better, listen. If your brain is telling you that a mistake was made, take a moment to begin analyzing what the mistake was and how to avoid it in the future.

Re-learning this type of focus and self-awareness will be key in the following chapters, and it will also be your savior in avoiding gaslighters—or at least, leaving early on in the relationship.

Forgive Yourself

At some point in this journey, you are going to find yourself asking 'why'. 'Why' you? "Why did this happen," you might say, or, "Why did they do it"? As mentioned in a previous chapter, these are valid questions. The problem is that a lot of these 'whys' will never be answered to a level that will bring you ultimate healing, because at this point, it is no longer about the person who gaslit you—it is about you.

It is about moving forward, forgiving yourself, and learning from your mistakes.

Hold On

Now, before going down a bad mental path, the above statement was in no way dismissing or writing off your experiences, trauma, or the fact that something awful has happened to you. Should the culprit be held responsible? Of course. The problem is that gaslighting is not always something that can be punishable by corporal law, and instead is something that has to be acknowledged, but then moved on from.

As mentioned previously, dwelling on the 'why' of the gaslighter may be a good place to start to help you recognize where things initially went wrong, or what behaviors you may have accidentally ignored or accepted. But that is as far as it can go.

Being able to let go of the 'why' then allows you to begin what this section is actually about forgiving yourself. At some point in this journey, you will begin to become frustrated that you allowed this situation to happen, that you did not leave sooner, or that you let the residual effects dictate so much of your life. While that self-anger should be given a space to be validated, it cannot control your healing process. You need to forgive yourself, the allowances you made, and the situation you were in, in order to move on.

Be Patient

Patience, as with anything, is key when it comes to recovery. This is not going to happen overnight. It may not even happen within a year, depending on the trauma and surrounding circumstances that you personally are facing. However, this is one of those times where you have got to trust the process and keep going (American Psychological Association et al., 2019).

However, please note that if things are not getting better, talk to a licensed professional.

Dealing with Your Trauma

Which brings us to the next step of recovery: dealing with your trauma. Normally, this is best done with a professional, such as a licensed therapist or counselor, as they will be able to learn your own psychological cues and help you forge new neural pathways in fighting old demons, trauma from your gaslighter, and creating new and healthy relationships. A lot of the steps for actually dealing with your trauma are similar to the steps for your recovery, but with one additional step.

Face Your Feelings

It is going to be hard, and avoidance is going to look so, so sweet. But avoiding your feelings through chosen ignorance, the use of substance, sleep, or isolation from loved ones/peripheral reminders, are going to make your mental and emotional stress actually worse overtime and keep you from healing and moving forward (American Psychological Association et al., 2019). Facing what you are feeling is like pulling a thorn from your hand, or mending a broken bone. It is going to hurt. There is no sugar coating it, but over time, as you become accustomed to facing your feelings, your feelings of being overwhelmed will lessen, and you may learn that you actually do not want to avoid your feelings anymore.

Ensuring Your Recovery Continues

At any point in the recovery journey, it is quite possible for a victim to stop or stay stuck at any of the particular steps. Reasons for this could vary: They could be too emotionally tired and need to take a legitimate break before moving forward, but then get too comfortable and refuse to continue. Victims could have experienced a high-level of emotional shut-down, where they are unable to continue recovery without extensive outside help. Or, victims could simply not want to continue forward because the future is unknown, and so far, their life experiences have not given them any promise of something good to hold onto and push forward.

If any of those scenarios fit your personal narrative, do not worry. There are always licensed professionals who are trained and more than willing to help you move forward at the pace you need, while also encouraging you to keep going.

But Why Should I Continue?

Or, maybe, you fall into the camp of wondering why you

should continue. Perhaps you have done most of the leg work and continuing on your road to recovery and ensuring that you have a safe place, etc., seems a bit unnecessary.

Let's put it another way: Without continuing to put in the hard work, even after the initial groundwork has been done, there is a very likely chance you could repeat the cycle. There is a reason successful addicts maintain strong groups of help, even when they have been sober for longer than they were an addict: Once your brain has made that particular pathway, it is always easy to fall back into it. That is not to say that your brain has been wired to seek out that type of abuse—not at all. However, your brain now knows how to function in that type of environment, which means that there is the likelihood that you may willingly, or accidentally, ignore the warning signs you have trained yourself to recognize. And the only way to truly avoid that is by having layers upon layers of fail-safes and accountability; and those can only be accessed if you personally continue on the journey of recovery.

You will not always need to check in with your safe person about each new relationship, job, or social network you create; but that might be a fail-safe that needs to be in place for now. You may not always need to go to a therapist, but it is something you need for right now. Only when you have truly reached a place of self-awareness, self-honesty, and self-acceptance, should you begin to reconsider altering the safety nets you have in place.

Going Forward

This brings up the "going forward" phase, or a few things to mention before continuing into the next segment and ensuing chapters. Going forward for this section will be to lay out very realistic possibilities of what your life may look like for the next little while, to ensure that you do not become the victim of another gaslighter.

Accountability

Accountability has gotten a bad reputation in society, as it is a word that is often prescribed for someone who is dealing with an addiction, or is given to someone who is living with an authoritative figure. Yet, if you think about it, accountability is actually a cornerstone of being a functioning person within any society. Whether you want to acknowledge it or not, you are in some way accountable for many things in your life. You are accountable for keeping your pet alive, your taxes paid, your money managed, your own self taken care of, etc. On top of that, you are probably accountable to more people than you would like to admit, even if it is for short periods of time.

Unconscious accountability partners come in many forms, like gym buddies, best friends who refuse to let you text your ex when you are lonely, reading partners, team members, or even fitness and nutrition coaches. When you think about it, our society has many forms of acceptable accountability partners, so you should never feel ashamed for having one to keep you safe as you recover from your gaslighting experience.

Good news is that it means incorporating it into your recovery from gaslighting will be easier. Bad news is that you will have to be honest with yourself and your accountability partner. Picking an accountability partner should not be hard, this person should be a safe person who has been aware of the entire scenario since you began your journey to recovery. Just remember that this person has to be someone who you will allow to call you out on suspicious behavior, without you getting defensive; or that this person will be able to call you out repeatedly, even if you get frustrated and attempt to ignore them. Additionally, your accountability partner has to be someone you respect and will listen to. If you do not listen to them, or at least have the mental awareness that you should listen to them, then they are no good to you as an accountability partner.

Safety Nets

Safety nets are predetermined actions to help keep you on the straight and narrow. For instance, if someone knows that they make bad decisions when they are lonely, they will often ask an accountability partner or a friend, to check in on them if they have not texted/contacted them in several days, or to ask questions if they begin to mention someone in a romantic way too often.

In regards to recovering from your gaslighting journey, you will need something similar. These safety nets will help you avoid making another relationship with a gaslighter, as well as act as a preventative measure to alert those in your close circle that something is wrong. It could be something as simple as having a code text word, or ensuring that you meet with one of your safe circles weekly. By this point, you may have a few ideas on what your safety nets should look like, but it is also a good idea to discuss options with a therapist, accountability partner, or trusted loved one.

Multiple Safe Circles

This brings up one of the final things you will need on your road to recovery: multiple safe circles. Safe circles refers to groups of people who are safe to you, and who are aware of what you are going through. A circle should never be more than one person (if at all possible), but can also be only two people. The reason you want more than one safe circle is so that you will have multiple options of people to call/text when you are having a bad day or things are going wrong.

It is unfair to ask only one person to be with you on this journey (but if that is all you have currently, along with a therapist, you can gradually increase your circles), because as you begin this journey you may rely on them a lot. Even if your safe person says that it is okay, have at least two back ups just in case. Good news is that as time goes on you can expand your safe circles to people who are unaware of your situation, but that you know would be safe if the need arose.

Remember, the whole point of having multiple safe circles is that these circles will act as a distraction or a reason to not engage with a gaslighter.

A Few Reminders and to Sum Up

This chapter was one of the meatier chapters, so we will do a brief summary and journal discussion to help orientate where you are emotionally, what you have to do, and how you can go about doing it.

First, you need to deal with your gaslighting experience by recovering from your trauma and dealing with your experience. Recovering from your trauma is where you are going to focus on your physical self. This step really emphasizes the actual physical steps you can take to begin distancing yourself from your gaslighter and creating a better physical space and life. Recovery deals with your grief, reconnecting with loved ones, and getting outside of the negative physical space and toxic environment you may have mentally created for yourself. Dealing with your trauma will include focusing on your inner self; and this step is often best done with help of a licensed individual or loved one. It is at this step that you will have to begin facing some hard truths about what you can do to begin avoiding going back into the situation you were just in.

Journaling

Now it is time to begin putting some of the thoughts that have been swimming in your head, onto a commitment of paper. Take a moment and begin writing down how you can enact your recovery steps, and begin to brainstorm what some of the requirements for dealing with your trauma will look like for you specifically. If you are already seeing a professional, take this list to them, and discuss options together. If you have a safe person, you could do that with them as well.

CHAPTER 5

How to Stop Gaslighting

It is all well and good to know how to deal with your past experiences, but there also comes the next steps of practicality: how to stop being gaslighted in the future.

What about just avoiding them entirely?

On the one hand it is possible to avoid gaslighters, however, having the intuition to do so will take years of work and/or becoming highly adept at noticing certain social scenarios the minute you walk into a room. While that is entirely possible, it takes years of work and an almost constant emotional meter on all social interactions that occur around you. So, while it is possible to avoid gaslighters, the concept of never meeting or engaging with one, is a bit trickier and will take some time to build up to.

But fear not! Hope is not lost. We simply need to shift our mindsets. Don't just cry out, "I will never come into contact with another gaslighter!" Begin to think about how you could help yourself spot a gaslighter earlier on in your interactions with them, and then what protocols you can follow to ensure that you will not be gaslit by them once they have been identified.

The Steps

Here are a few steps to help get you started.

Minimize Contact

It is important when you have spotted a gaslighter to minimize how often you see or interact with them on a daily basis (Greenberg, 2021). Remember: One of the ways gaslighters are able to work is by being with you daily and subconsciously wearing down your inhibitions so that they are able to make their moves.

Well, how could I possibly do that in the workplace or in my family?

Simple, by instigating boundaries and being polite, but also distant. Think of it this way: You have probably been in situations where you have had to coexist with people that you did not like. This scenario is just like that, only this time, you are going to have to take extra steps to help ensure that you are emotionally and mentally safe, as well as polite and courteous so that the discrediting tactics gaslighters are so fond of using, cannot happen.

In order to help you understand how this could look in various situations, brief run-downs will be given for each relationship that has been discussed in this book. Remember: This section is how to stop gaslighting and is not dealing with the relationship that got you to read this book in the first place.

Romantic Relationships

This one is pretty easy. If you believe that the person you are in a romantic relationship with is a gaslighter, tell them that it is over and move on. If you have just started dating, or have not been dating that long, breaking ties will be relatively easy.

Friendships or Peers

The same goes for friendships or peer relationships where you are starting to notice unhealthy gaslighting signs. Minimizing your contact in these relationships could be as simple as no longer talking to that person, or, by simply not seeing/talking/engaging with that person often.

For the latter example, let's say that a new peripheral friend has been introduced into a social group that you are closely linked to. Over a few interactions you have begun to notice that the new person may not be who they appear to be, and they seem to have hidden agendas and are using gaslighting techniques on several members in the group. Before helping those who are being gaslit (remember, when it comes to any form of abuse, it is important to help yourself before you help others— helping others before you have your own safeguards in place will help no one in the long term), you decide to begin minimizing your contact with the gaslighter. You stop going to every single group hang-out, and instead begin to invest time and energy in other social circles. You tell someone who is not in that circle what you think is happening, to begin establishing a third party perspective, and you make sure that any interaction you have with the gaslighter is public knowledge (e.g. you do not meet them for one-on-one coffee dates, ensure that the texts they send you are screenshot and saved, and make sure that you are not left alone with them when you go out with the group). Only once those safeguards and habits are in place, do you then begin to help those who have become the gaslighters victims.

In the above example, by ensuring your own safety and mental health, you are then in a prime position to help the main victims of the gaslighting. Yes, it seems wrong to let them suffer, but to be honest, the steps that you would need to take to ensure that you are not a victim are not only more important, but can be done in a relatively short time period if you already have your own safeguards in place—see why continuing your recovery can be useful?

The Workplace

Minimizing your contact with a boss or coworker becomes a bit trickier. Thankfully, the ways that you can protect yourself against a gaslighter will help ensure that you will still be safe, even if you have to have weekly meetings, or one-on-one manager meetings with the gaslighter.

When it comes to your coworkers, the same steps for friends or peers can be applied, and you will be able to create a healthy work environment for yourself. A boss, on the other hand, takes a little bit more follow-through. Sadly, if your manager is a gaslighter, there is not a lot of 'minimizing' contact that you can do right away. Instead, you will have to be diligent in gathering information, talking to trusted third parties, and getting Human Resources involved to resolve that situation.

Family Scenarios

If you notice gaslighting in your immediate family, minimizing contact if you still live at home may be difficult, and, similar to how to handle a boss, you will have to gather information and perform more of a confrontation with safe-people backing you. Followed by minimizing how much you see or interact with the person. If you do not live with that person, minimizing contact becomes easy, since you can choose if you answer phone calls, texts, or emails; you could even change your lock if they have a key to your home.

For removed family members like grandparents, aunts, uncles, or cousins, the same technique applies. Thankfully, in most scenarios you most likely do not live with that person, and therefore, you can choose how you want to minimize contact. If you only see that person in family gatherings, it becomes a personal choice on how you want to go about it. You could ensure that you are never alone in the room with them, that you bring a trusted third party to family events so that the narrative can become questioned, or even not go if it truly makes you uncomfortable.

Neighbors

When it comes to your neighbors, minimizing contact is possibly the easiest, since you probably have little contact with them to begin with. Instead, just focus on gathering evidence and getting the right authority figures involved if you need them to be.

Be True to Yourself

Another way to ensure that you do not fall into the trap of a gaslighter is to be true to yourself, meaning, having a clear and concise picture of who you are (Greenberg, 2021; Staff, 2020). If you are confident in who you are, and what you are or are not capable of, then you will know that anything a gaslighter says about you is not true. There is a saying from Ann Landers that goes, "People of integrity expect to be believed. If not, they let time prove them right." (Landers, n.d.). While it may sound a little silly, and there is a strong possibility that it could lead to a lonely and long road, that is exactly what it means to be true to yourself here. When you are interacting with a gaslighter, you have to be the person with integrity.

You have to believe that sooner or later, you will be proved right (and you can quietly gather evidence to ensure that you are proven right). What this also means is that you will not engage when the gaslighter attempts to anger or bait you into a debate about yourself, or the narrative that they (the gaslighter) are attempting to spin (Greenberg, 2021; Staff, 2020).

Keep Interactions Simple

If you absolutely have to be in contact with a gaslighter, keep your interactions simple and to the point of why you must engage with them (Greenberg, 2021; Staff, 2020). This coincides with minimizing contact and being true to yourself: You are not being rude by not engaging—although you will have to ensure that your words and tone are polite—you are making sure that your mental health and personal safety are coming first. Now, that does not mean that you have to say it that way when the gaslighter confronts you on why you are behaving a certain way—and let's be honest, they will, because they will notice when someone is not playing their game. What you can say as a response is, "I prefer to keep our interactions professional, and only discuss what is needed for this project/team/etc."

By saying it in such a way you are neither engaging in the bait the gaslighter has used, nor are you being discourteous or dishonest in why you are minimizing contact with them.

Keep Strong Contact with Positive Outside Influences

There is no denying that our friends, safe people, and therapists (if you have one), are the cornerstone of our sanity; especially when manipulative or abusive people come into our lives. Even if the contact you have with a gaslighter is minimal, even if you have cut them out of your life, keeping your loved ones up to date on what is happening is a great way to ensure accountability, as well as not creating a backdoor for a gaslighter to attack you another way.

As said previously, there is a good chance that your gaslighter—or almost any gaslighter for that matter— does not have a master plan for you specifically. Sure, television shows, books, and Hollywood have put it into our heads that more and more sociopaths exist (and they may not be wrong), but even in those scenarios the sociopaths are caught or stopped by maintaining transparency with those we love and trust. Hiding something from our loved and trusted ones honestly does not do anyone any favors. In fact, it can often be more harmful than you think. Keeping something from the ones that you are accountable to, and go to help for, actually stops them from legitimately helping you in the journey. Help that is given in the moment, based on one facet of a scenario, is not always the best form of help. It may seem tedious and unnecessary, but keeping those that already know about your current or previous gaslighting instances, should be kept up to date with future interactions with other gaslighters. This interaction and knowledge will help them help you, as well as enable them to give you the best advice possible.

It Is not You

This was said continuously throughout the book, however, when meeting a new gaslighter it is important to remember that it is not you. Gaslighters exist everywhere in the world, and meeting more than one has nothing to do with bad luck, bad circumstance, or even your character or personality—unless a licensed therapist has said otherwise. Instead, all it means is that you simply are aware that something is wrong.

You Do not Need to Win

The problem for many people when they know that they are in contact with a gaslighter, is that an innate sense of wrong-ness starts to get irked. It is irksome that they get away with it, it is annoying that so many people bow to their whims, and it is absolutely frustrating that they are not confronted and forced to change—that you know of. Those feelings are completely understandable, and honestly, it frustrates everyone.

The thing is: Engaging in a battle of wills with a gaslighter, even if it is with the intent of winning or putting them in their place, is exactly what the gaslighter wants, because you are now in close contact with them (Greenberg, 2021; Staff, 2020). Even if you personally go into those interactions with a "war mentality", the gaslighter is still getting what they want; and do you really want to give them what they want?

Gather Evidence

This has been said in many of the previous steps, but it deserves its own little blurb here: Keep the evidence of the gaslighters' actions if cutting them out of your life is not possible. This evidence will come in handy, and it will also allow you to recognize the little ticks and tricks that particular gaslighter has. Additionally, this evidence will help make the gaslighters actions clear to you, in case you begin to have any doubts (Greenberg, 2021; Staff, 2020). Going back and re-reading and analyzing events can help you realize if you are truly in contact with a gaslighter (in case you have been trying to convince yourself otherwise) and will help your third party gain perspective on what your next moves should be.

Going Forward

All of these steps, signs, and to-do lists make this sound like a long process, and unfortunately, it is. But it will also be completely worth it, because it will help you create a mental, physical, and emotional safe space. Nothing worth having is gotten easily (unless you are a prodigy), and your mental health is one of those things.

Having a healthy and gaslighter-free space is completely worth the effort it will take to get there, and these steps will put you on the road to greatness. So, now, take a moment and go back through all of the steps that were given to you and begin to look at your own life and lingering doubts about any other relationships. Could these steps be used anywhere else?

CHAPTER 6

Building a Healthy Relationship

Building healthy relationships with other people may seem impossible at the moment, but don't worry, it's not. What you are feeling right now is most likely an overwhelming sense of every single emotion possible, because this book has woken you up to feelings, circumstances, and brought changes to you that you may have wanted and needed; but they will still take a lot of effort to enact. Thankfully, in this chapter, we will discuss how to build healthy relationships using everything you have learned so far. This will include: figuring out how to get back to your normal (or how to create a new normal if that is applicable to you), actively healing from your trauma as you continue to live life, and how gaslighting might have affected your other relationships and what healing those wounds may look like.

Just like any other part of this book, figuring out how to build healthy relationships with others and creating a new normal is going to take time, but thankfully there are two steps you can do before or during your healing journey. These are: figuring out your new normal, and analyzing your relationships.

Before going any further, it is important to say here that you can do this. Everything that has been discussed so far, and will be discussed for the rest of this book, are things that are completely doable if you are willing and have a healthy support system. It will be hard, but countless others have done it before you, so you are not alone in anything you are feeling.

Getting Back to Normal

So what does "getting back to normal" really mean? It means that you are now ready to begin living life without your gaslighter. No, that does not mean abandoning the trauma, protocols, or awareness that you have hopefully gained by this point. In reality, what this chapter is about is how to tie everything you have learned into mental packages that you can use as you continue to simply live your life.

Figuring out what was normal for you will really depend on how much you remember of your life pre-gaslighting. For some of you, those memories will be relatively easy to picture, and for others there may not even be a healthy past to rely on. Each scenario will be covered.

For both scenarios of getting back to normal, it is important that you pick models that align with the intrinsic knowledge of yourself. If you know that you are not an adrenaline junkie, making extreme sports a part of your "new normal" is not a good idea. There is a fine line between being adventurous or trying something new, and doing something that could be seen as a way to avoid actually making your new normal. A great way to determine this is to ask yourself if this is something you actually have always wanted or could want, or if this is something that sounds fun because you really do not want to focus on finding the new normal.

The not too Distant Past

If you are able to remember what your life was like before your gaslighter, re-creating a healthier version of that past to merge into your new normal will be relatively easy. Well, easy in the way that you know what you are aiming for. The joy of forging a "new normal" is that you will be able to cherry pick what you liked and what you did not like, and create your new normal off of those attributes.

Think about the few years of your life when you were truly happy before your gaslighter. What did you do for fun? Who were your friends? What were your hobbies? Where did you live? What were you doing for money? Think about the key points of your life that your gaslighter has affected, and what they were like before. Now think about what parts of that life you loved, and what you do not want to recreate—gaslighter aside. If that means you move to another city, do it. If that means you find another job, do it. If that means you call up an old friend, apologize, and try to re-establish that friendship, do it.

Chances are, if your gaslighter was able to gain full control over your life, you may have to apologize and put your ego and possibly your trauma "to the side" in order to re-open some doors that you purposefully closed. This will be easier with personal relationships, as the foundation of trust, acceptance, and openly sharing traumatic events will have already been established. Previous jobs on the other hand, may have to be something that you let go of and try to recreate in a different way. Before going any further it is important to note that in this segment putting your ego or trauma "to the side" does not mean to excuse what has happened to you, or to not share it. It means that you will have to be okay with the people you have hurt expressing their own hurt to you. Now, if those people dismiss your current trauma and what has happened— get out. That is a sign of gaslighting.

But if that person is genuinely upset that those events happened to you, but still wants you to know that your actions hurt them as well, that is unfortunately the price that has to be paid to re-establish the relationship.

Making Something out of Nothing

For those of you that do not remember what life was like before your gaslighter began to isolate and gaslight you, then you have several decisions to make. Begin to wonder about things like: Where do I really want to live?

What do I want to do? What does my ideal life look like in terms of: friends, hobbies, pets, etc. Now is the time for you to live the life you have wanted. Without your gaslighter, the world is truly your oyster. Depending on what you want it may take some time—and a lot of dedication—to get there, but there is honestly very little standing in your way now. If you want to have a thriving social life that goes out every weekend, time to go to some places you enjoy hanging out (or using an app) and attempting to build that social network. If you are someone who wants to become more creative on a daily basis, time to find creative circles that have drop-in nights, or night classes you can take.

It may take a little bit of out-of-the-box thinking, but you really are able to make the life you want. However, you may need more help than those who have experienced a life they were already happy with. Do not be afraid to ask for help, or to lean on your loved ones or a therapist to help you find resources and the wherewithal to get there. That is what they are there for, and you can truly do it. Do not give up.

Whatever You Choose, Be Realistic

Regardless of how you are going to find your "new

normal", make sure that you pick models that include acknowledging the past trauma you have undergone. Ignoring your past trauma will do you no favors. This trauma and what you have gone through or are going through, will define parts of yourself that you may not be aware of. Be open to those changes, and if you are unhappy with the end result, find safe ways to combat that —either with the help of a therapist or loved one.

Whatever you choose, you need to be realistic. This is a time of great opportunity, but great opportunity can also be where some people's dreams go to die. Not because they do not want them to happen, but because people get overwhelmed, give up, or pick something that is too complex for the simplistic steps they want to use to get there. You need to set yourself up for success, not failure.

Your Other Relationships and Gaslighting

This section is honestly going to require a lot of introspection and honesty, because here, we are going to discuss how to analyze any correlations between your gaslighting relationship, and ones that you have still kept. Here, we will cover two aspects of how gaslighting has affected your relationships with other people. First, we are going to discuss the relationships you were able to maintain while being gaslit; and second, we will discuss how to create healthy and new relationships without letting your past trauma directly influence new relational choices in unhealthy ways.

Your Current Relationships

Now that you are armed with new information on how to handle the relationships in your life that actually are based on gaslighting and extreme negativity in your life, it is time to consider other relationships you have. Not just to make sure that there are not subtle gaslighting behaviors in those relationships, but also how to move forward with the new knowledge you have, and how to create healthier, more encouraging relationships with everyone around you.

If you are able to maintain strong relationships while being gaslighted, or if there are relationships that you can return to easily, then you are actually in an amazing place, because you will have safe circles and safe people immediately. However, that does not mean that your time as a victim did not go unnoticed, or that did not affect those relationships.

Wait, What?

Yes, it is true. There is a good chance that when you thought you were being stoic, hiding your feelings and what was happening—or so deep in your own isolation and depression that you could not possibly notice how it affected your other relationships—those other people definitely noticed something. They may have even attempted to reach out to you, and you may have engaged, or you may have ignored. Yes, you are the victim, and yes, they most likely will come from a place of understanding when you tell them. However, you also have to recognize—as was mentioned in the last section—that you may have also hurt them while you were hurting (remember: Hurt people hurt people).

What this means is that when it comes to your current relationships there are two steps to follow: first is to reconnect, and the second is to heal.

Reconnecting

Reconnecting with old relationships is something that has been discussed at various points within this book, but what does that look like? Thankfully with the help of modern technology it is actually really simple: You call or text them. That's it.

It can literally be a message asking to meet for coffee, and that you need to talk to them. Now, while you are reaching out, you need to recognize that they may not want to meet you right away, and you may have to do some explaining via message in order to get them to meet face-to-face. While that sucks, it is possible, and those people are completely within their rights to do that. Depending on how isolated you were, you may have deeply hurt those people, and while the love of our loved ones can go quite far, there are sometimes when they need to be reassured that you had a reason for acting the way you did.

Once you have been able to reconnect with that friend, you will need to let them also explain their own feelings to you, after you have explained your absence or neglect. Yes, you read that right: neglect. There is absolutely no way that neglecting a friend or family member diminishes what happened to you. But remember that section on emotional validation, and the constant reminders of how our emotions are perceived? Just because you were abused does not negate the potential harm you accidentally inflicted on others. Now, that is not to say that you need to open the meeting with you apologizing, because that is completely incorrect. What it does mean is that, if that person has brought their grievances to your attention, you may have to apologize. And you have to be open to them telling you that you hurt them.

Heal Together

Now that you have reconnected with past relationships it is time to create a journey of healing together—it will have some similarities to your own personal healing journey. Part of that difference is that you and those relationships need to establish together what you and they can put into place to avoid what happened in the past. This could be a code word, an extra level of understanding, or even the ability to extend more grace towards the other. Whatever you need to implement, as long as it is healthy and creates a safe and healthy place for you both, is what you need to do to help that relationship begin to thrive again.

Next is something that will come naturally: beginning to heal the relationship through time and interaction. In all honesty, there is nothing like hanging with a loved one after a healthily resolved fight. It sounds corny, but it is true. The rush of happy emotions and brain chemicals from resolving even minimal conflict with someone you love, will go a long way in re-establishing the bond you had once shared with that person. Bask in it. Grow in it. Use it. Use this new-found connection to stem the feelings of emptiness the gaslighter has left behind. Remember what it was like to be in that relationship again. Begin to build newer, better, and stronger memories together. After what you have been through, you deserve and need it.

New Relationships

Creating new relationships may seem a little scary at first, especially if your gaslighter began as a new relationship that went terribly wrong. Good news is you do not necessarily have to do this right away, you can take some time re-establishing old relationships and building your new life, before actively seeking out new relationships.

But do not let that phase of getting comfortable in your old/new life last too long. If you become too comfortable and dependent on old relationships, you may unknowingly increase your fear and anxiety over creating new relationships, which honestly could have the potential to be just as good as what you have now.

If you are worried about encountering another

gaslighting relationship, do not worry, that is why the previous chapters on how to spot, how to heal, how to confront, and how to stop gaslighting were written. Using all of that information will help you minimize any contact you may have with potential gaslighters, and will become easy over time. The biggest thing you will have to work on, is fighting the newly ingrained fears you have about gaslighters. So here are a few reminders:

Not Everyone is a Gaslighter

If you were in a long relationship with a gaslighter, and if people were unaware or ignorant of your trauma, then it may be really hard to believe that everyone you meet is not a gaslighter. Truthfully, they are not. You may encounter some unfortunate circumstances where certain individuals have not been educated or updated their language to no longer include gaslighting phrases, but not everyone will be one. It will be hard, but you have got to remember this when meeting new people. Even asking your safe person, close friend, loved one, or therapist to help remind you, could go a long way in combating that trauma.

You Are not Damaged

It is normal for trauma victims to believe that they are now damaged goods and unable to create healthy relationships instead of toxic ones. That is what this entire book is for: to give you the tools to begin creating healthy relationships with other people, including the one you have with yourself. You are not damaged. You are not unable to make good relationships. And you are worthy of them.

It Is Okay to Make Mistakes

If you somehow get into another relationship with a gaslighter, or into a different kind of toxic relationship (it unfortunately happens), or if you are unable to forgive yourself for willingly going into your past toxic relationship—recognize that mistakes happen. You are only human, and it is okay for you to make mistakes. Yes, it sucks that the mistake happened, that you lost time, that this happened to you, and that you are now dealing with trauma no one should ever have to deal with. But it was a mistake. It does not define you, and it is okay that you made it.

Please note: There is a big difference between the situation you were in as being 'okay' and it was 'okay' that you accidentally got into it. That situation was never 'okay', and you most likely had to lie to yourself to believe that it was. But it is 'okay' that you accidentally got into it, because you did not knowingly choose something toxic. Even if it was known, you most likely did it out of your own trauma or hurt. Mistakes happen. Accept it, and learn to be okay with it.

This could also be a good topic for your therapist if this is hard for you to grasp or establish in your self-talks.

The World Is Scary, but People Do not Have to Be

Yes, the world is a big and scary place, and honestly so are some of the people in it. Such is the fate of being human and understanding the motives and characters of others. But not everyone that is in this world is scary. In order to create a new normal, to figure out how to build healthy relationships, and honestly, how to get over your gaslighting trauma, you are going to have to begin to acknowledge that not everyone in this world is scary, and some people will be worth meeting.

Just Do It

It sounds awful, it really does. But the only way to face your fear is to, well… do it. No, that does not mean to go and touch a snake if you are deathly afraid of them, or that you should jump off a cliff because you are afraid of heights. Those fears are slightly rational, but your fear of creating new bonds with new humans—while totally understandable—are not entirely rational. Mankind was meant to crave and be in a community. Please do not let your gaslighter rob you of that.

Letting the fear of "what if it is another gaslighter" rule your life, is intrinsically letting your past gaslighter win. Please do not let them do that. Defy what they have done to you, and begin to forge into new relationships. You will have past relationships, friends, loved ones, and licensed professionals, to lean on and help you with this. But please, do not forget that life is worth living, including making new friends, finding that new job, or finding that new significant other, or even, making your own family.

Conclusion

And now we have come to the end of our journey on how to understand gaslighters. Hopefully by reading this book you now understand what gaslighting is, how it works, how it slips into everyday life, the signs and stages of recognizing gaslighters, how to handle them, how to deal with your trauma, and how to move forward after being gaslighted.

As you begin your own personalized phases of healing and moving past this, remember that you can do this. It will not be easy, and it will be a lot of effort, but the effort will be well worth it. At the end of this journey, you will be able to recognize gaslighters and live a life free of them.

And while it may seem incredibly repetitive, let's end this book on one of the strongest reminders you will need throughout this journey: It was not your fault, you do not deserve this, you can heal from it, and you can move on with your life. Prove your gaslighter wrong the right way. Build a healthy, successful, and happy life—without them.

Thank You

Before you leave, I'd just like to say, thank you so much for purchasing my book.

I spent many days and nights working on this book so I could finally put this in your hands.

So, before you leave, I'd like to ask you a small favor.

Would you please consider posting a review on the platform? Your reviews are one of the best ways to support indie authors like me, and every review counts. Your feedback will allow me to continue writing books just like this one, so let me know if you enjoyed it and why. I read every review and I would love to hear from you.

To leave a review simply scan the QR code below or go to Amazon.com, go to "Your Orders" and then find it under "Digital Orders".

Scan the QR Code Below to Leave a Review:

References

American Psychological Association, Youn, S. J., & Halfond, R. (2019, October 30). *How to cope with traumatic stress.* American Psychological Association. https://www.apa.org/topics/trauma/stress

Cloud, H. (2019, October 27). *Dr. Henry Cloud | What are boundaries?* Youtube. https://www.youtube.com/watch?v=7AW9ENJIt 1o

Colino, S. (2021, October 25). *Gaslighting in families: Signs of gaslighting parents* (J. Kim, Ed.). Psycom.net - Mental Health Treatment Resource since 1996. https://www.psycom.net/gaslighting-parents-families

Friedman, W. J. (n.d.). *Feelings are authentic and valid — Perceptions and beliefs are suspect - wellness, disease prevention, and stress reduction information.* MentalHelp. Retrieved February 8, 2022, from https://www.mentalhelp.net/blogs/feelings-are-authentic-and-valid-perceptions-and-beliefs-are-suspect/

Gaslighting | Psychology today Canada. (n.d.). Psychology Today. Retrieved February 10, 2022, from https://www.psychologytoday.com/ca/basics/gaslighting

Gillihan, S. (2018, November 18). *When is it gaslighting and when is it not?* Psychology Today. https://www.psychologytoday.com/us/blog/think-act-be/201811/when-is-it-gaslighting-and-when-is-it-not

Gordon, S. (2022, January 5). *Understanding the manipulative behaviors toxic people use to control.* Verywell Mind; Very Well Mind. https://www.verywellmind.com/is-someone-gaslighting-you-4147470

Greenberg, M. (2021, June 30). 5 go-to tactics of gaslighters, and how to resist them | psychology today Canada. Psychology Today. https://www.psychologytoday.com/ca/blog/the-mindful-self-express/202106/5-go-tactics-gaslighters-and-how-resist-them

Huizen, J. (2020, July 14). *What is gaslighting? Examples and how to respond.* Medicalnewstoday. https://www.medicalnewstoday.com/articles/gaslighting

Landers, A. (n.d.). *A quote from a sequence for academic writing.* Goodreads. Retrieved February 18, 2022, from https://www.goodreads.com/quotes/9861011-people-with-integrity-expect-to-be-believed-if-not-they

Leaf, C. (2019, January 21). *Episode #63: Using your discomfort zones to regulate your thinking and improve your mental health.* Youtube.

https://www.youtube.com/watch?v=zY7qVegEK
Bk

Merriam-Webster. (n.d.). *Definition of codependency*. Merriam-Webster. Retrieved February 12, 2022, from https://www.merriam-webster.com/dictionary/codependency

Moore, A. (2019, March 2). *Abuse prevention: how to turn off the gaslighters*. The Guardian. https://www.theguardian.com/lifeandstyle/2019/mar/02/abuse-prevention-how-to-turn-off-the-gaslighters

Moore, K. (2021, June 22). *Declared insane for speaking up: The dark American history of silencing women through psychiatry*. Time. https://time.com/6074783/psychiatry-history-women-mental-health/

Ni, P. (2013, April 30). *7 stages of gaslighting in a relationship*. Psychology Today. https://www.psychologytoday.com/ca/blog/communication-success/201704/7-stages-gaslighting-in-relationship

Ni, P. (2017, February 15). *8 signs that someone is in a relationship with a gaslighter* | Psychology today Canada. Psychology Today.com. https://www.psychologytoday.com/ca/blog/communication-success/201702/8-signs-someone-is-in-relationship-gaslighter

Ni, P. (2020, July 20). 7 signs of gaslighting at the workplace | Psychology today Canada. Psychology Today. https://www.psychologytoday.com/ca/blog/communication-success/202007/7-signs-gaslighting-the-workplace

Pan, M. (2021, July 10). *How to identify an emotionally safe person. hello, love.* Medium. https://medium.com/hello-love/how-to-identify-an-emotionally-safe-person-8b6a49169

Patrik, W. (2021, July 3). *Why do domestic violence victims return to abusers?* Psychology Today. https://www.psychologytoday.com/ca/blog/why-bad-looks-good/202107/why-do-domestic-violence-victims-return-abusers

Penn State. (2019, September 30). *People with anxiety may strategically choose worrying over relaxing.* ScienceDaily. https://www.sciencedaily.com/releases/2019/09/190930114737.htm

Salters-Pednault, K. (2021, April 21). *What you can do to help others feel validated.* Verywell Mind. https://www.verywellmind.com/what-is-emotional-validation-425336

Sarkis, S. (2019, July 12). Rebuilding after a gaslighting or narcissistic relationship. Psychology Today. . https://www.psychologytoday.com/ca/blog/here-there-and-everywhere/201907/rebuilding-after-gaslighting-or-narcissistic-relationship

Staff, N. (2020, September 10). *What is gaslighting? Confronting the emotional abuse.* Northpoint Recovery's Blog. https://www.northpointrecovery.com/blog/gaslighting-examples-effects-confront-abuse/

Sweeton, J. (2017, March 13). *How to heal the traumatized brain.* Psychology Today. https://www.psychologytoday.com/ca/blog/workings-well-being/201703/how-heal-the-traumatized-brain

Made in United States
Troutdale, OR
11/02/2024